SHASHI DESHPANDE'S NOVELS

A Feminist Study

SIDDHARTHA SHARMA

ATLANTIC
PUBLISHERS & DISTRIBUTORS

Published by

 **ATLANTIC**
PUBLISHERS & DISTRIBUTORS
B-2, Vishal Enclave, Opp. Rajouri Garden,
New Delhi-110027
Phones : 25413460, 25429987, 25466842

Sales Office
7/22, Ansari Road, Darya Ganj,
New Delhi-110002
Phones : 23273880, 23275880, 23280451
Fax : 91-11-23285873
web : www.atlanticbooks.com
e-mail : info@atlanticbooks.com

Copyright © Atlantic Publishers and Distributors, 2005

ISBN 81-269-0385-6

Printed in India
at Nice Printing Press, Delhi

PREFACE

Shashi Deshpande is a leading women novelist on the Indian literary horizon with seven novels and four collections of short stories to her credit. She has also received the prestigious Sahitya Akademi Award for her novel, *That Long Silence* (1989). But unfortunately she has not yet received the critical attention she deserves.

The present study aims at evaluating Deshpande's potential as a serious writer genuinely concerned with women's issues. Trapped between tradition and modernity, her women protagonists undergo great mental trauma in their quest for identity before they affirm themselves. A close study of her novels will reveal as to how well and how far she has been able to voice their concerns.

Roots and Shadows, her first novel, depicts the agony and suffocation experienced by the protagonist Indu in a male-dominated and tradition-bound society. *The Dark Holds No Terrors,* her second novel, is all about male ego wherein the male refuses to play a second fiddle role in marriage. *That Long Silence,* her third novel, is about self-doubts and fears which Jaya undergoes till she affirms herself. *The Binding Vine,* her fourth novel, deals with the personal tragedy of the protagonist Urmi to focus attention on victims like Kalpana and Mira—victims of man's lust and woman's helplessness. In her novel, *A Matter of Time,* Deshpande for the first time enters into the metaphysical world of philosophy. It is about three women from three generations of the same family and the way they cope with the tragedy that overwhelms them. *Small Remedies,* her latest novel, is about Savitribai Indorekar, the aging doyenne of Hindustani music, who avoids marriage and home to pursue her genius.

Excepting a handful of critical articles and reviews, in addition to 'Image of Women' kind of books, a full-fledged study of her novels has not been evaluated even after two decades of the appearance of her first novel, *Roots and Shadows* (1983). Since, she is a woman writer with a broad humanistic outlook, a threadbare exposition of her novels from the viewpoint of feminism is rendered imminent.

SIDDHARTHA SHARMA

CONTENTS

1
INTRODUCTION

◆

The book attempts to make a feminist study of Shashi Deshpande's novels. As an author of the '70s and '80s, she mirrors a realistic picture of the contemporary middle-class, educated, urban Indian woman. At a glance, her novels appear to be products of feminism, thereby lending a fresh perspective for critical analysis. The book not only projects the miserable plight of the contemporary middle-class, urban Indian woman but also analyses how their lot hasn't changed much through the centuries even in the twentieth century.

But before going into the feminist world of Shashi Deshpande, for a fair evaluation of her mind and art, an exposition is rendered imminent as to how the patriarchal and male-dominated Indian society looks [down] upon women and also the straitjacketed roles it has defined for them.

The women have been traditionally characterized as ideally warm, gentle and submissive, who are to be kept in subordination to the male members of the family. Manu declares:

> Day and night, women must be kept in subordination to the males of the family: in childhood to the father, in youth to her husband, in old age to her sons. [...] Even though the husband be destitute of virtue and seeks pleasure elsewhere, he must be worshipped as god.[1]

Women were denied the right to study the Vedas, and were bracketed with sinners and slaves. The code of Manu was so rigorously observed that the role of women was confined to the family, and thus they were denied rights equal to man. Although her lot in the family kept changing with the times, but it invariably remained an inferior one. Still she is hardly given much freedom. Shantha Krishnaswamy comments on the general lot of women thus:

> She is a creature who as a child is sold off to strangers for a bridal price, or when she grows up, serves as a supplier of dowry for her husband's family, or who as a widow, in a final act of obliteration immolates herself on her dead husband's funeral pyre to be acclaimed as 'Sita-Savitri', as an immortal.[2]

The early decades of the 20th century witnessed an improvement in the women's lot, which was the outcome of the movements of Raja Ram Mohan Roy and Jotiba Phule. A major change was effected by Mahatma Gandhi's emphasis on women's participation in his non-violent movement. In an article on Gandhi entitled "Not by Faith Alone," Ramachandra Guha observes:

> Woman is the companion, Gandhiji affirmed as early as 1918 with equal mental capacities and she has the same right of freedom and liberty. He (Gandhi) dismissed the ideas put forward by Manu as an interpolation and if it was not an interpolation, he could only say that in Manu's days, women did not have the status they deserved.[3]

Simultaneous with it was the introduction of Western liberal education that forced new values of life upon women. Legally, she has been given equal right with man, the submissive and gentle nature of women embedded deeply into their psyche did not disturb the male-dominance in the family. The male mentality is so shaped that it cannot adjust to the notion of woman being equal to man.

Despite equal opportunities of education and economic independence, women remained a victim of domestic injustice within the family, and other legal rights outside. Despite the universally acknowledged fact that women perform on par with man physically and mentally, they have been denied the freedom to express their feelings, thoughts and anguish. The women have been working indoors and outdoors, but their services remain unrecognized. Although the lot of women in the family and society has changed with the times for the better, but remained invariably inferior to those of men.

The last quarter of the 19th century witnessed the emergence of some great women writers like Toru Dutt, Mrs Ghoshal, Sorabji Cornelia and Krupabal Sathianathan. K.S. Ramamurti, in his book *Rise of the Indian Novel in English*, says, "it [their works] was qualitatively superior to those of many others who wrote before and after them."[4]

The movements of Raja Ram Mohan Roy and Mahatma Gandhi proved a great relief to women as they were brought out of the tyranny of the social evils. Still the number of women enjoying considerable freedom was very meagre. For the majority of women, subordination to men and misery was synonymous. The battle for emancipation was taken over by a few educated women, and they turned writers. The motive was to voice their own bitter experiences as women with a view to influencing the society and effecting social reforms. Professor John B. Alphonso-Karkala in his book *Indo-English Literature of the Nineteenth Century* writes:

> They tried to tell the world the obstacles women faced and the disadvantages they suffered in an orthodox Hindu world. These women writers struggled to give form and shape to their autobiographical accounts, which attracted publishers, both in India and abroad.[5]

The ideal image of woman like the traditional Sita or Savitri was gradually replaced by the realistic one, i.e. the frustrated and alienated one. The introduction of liberal English education not only brought significant changes in the middle-class life-style but also raised a consciousness of freedom in the minds of women. This only led to a romantic desire for a freedom that wasn't easy to come by. The women writers, thus, used this conflict between tradition and modernity. It was a portrayal of women facing the conflicts and problems issuing from the fusion of the traditional and modern values. The transition from the old to the new; from the traditional to the modern affect both the sexes, but the fair sex gets the worst of it—the crisis of value adaptation being the more excruciating. The modern age has left woman confused between the opposing forces of modernity and tradition, and they find it difficult to reconcile between their romantic aspirations and the realities of life. It is a conflict between a personal fulfilment of desires and their duty towards family and children.

Thus, most of the woman novelists took up the theme of the problem of adjustment, and they are shown adjusting themselves to the ground reality. Earlier the problems of women were more of an emotional nature due to her attachment to home and family. But with her increasing consciousness as an individual, she has begun to assert herself within the family and outside it as well. A society conditioned to the age-old patriarchal mindset opposes and rejects such deviation from the established social norms, and his opposition to her quest for identity and selfhood becomes a cause of her seemingly impossible struggle. Although there are many women forums voicing their concern, but the going seems tough.

The road ahead is rugged and full of hurdles in a chauvinistic society where most women wouldn't support the movement for fear of losing the little freedom they enjoy in the confinement of the four-walls. Sushila Singh rightly observes:

> Human experience for centuries has been synonymous with the masculine experience with the result that the collective image of humanity has been one-sided and incomplete. Woman has not been defined as a subject in her own right but merely has an entity that concern man either in his real life or his fantasy life.[6]

Since the inception of the feminist movement in the 1960s in the West, much has been written on women, but much still remains to be done to reflect the injustices meted out to women and also to rid the male-psyche of the prejudices and misconceptions regarding them.

Alexander Dumas, the nineteenth century French dramatist, was the first to use the term "feminism" for the movement for women's political rights. Later it spread across the world to secure complete rights for women—political, social, economic and educational. The movement went from strength to strength and, by the end of the twentieth century, made the complacent society to think anew about the age-old distorted beliefs. The movement could not make much headway in Indian society steeped in religious belief, superstitions and tradition. Though, of late, feminism does seem to have begun influencing a cross-section of the Indian society. Some few Indian writers in English have challenged the hitherto unchallenged man-woman relationship.

Ibsen heralded the idea of woman's emancipation with his character Nora in *A Doll's House*. But it was Simone de Beauvoir's book *The Second Sex*, first published in French in the year 1949, that sowed the seeds for a women's movement. It won great acclaim as a feminist book when its English translation was made accessible to the world. She successfully shatters the myth of femininity and shows how, deprived of their social, economic and political rights, they remain relegated to the background. Despite their great contribution, they are dubbed as the weaker sex.

Despite their numerical strength they are told that their femininity is in danger. Simone de Beauvoir writes:

> All agree in recognising the fact that female exists in the human species; today as always they make up about one half of humanity. And yet we are told that femininity is in danger; we are exhorted to be women, remain women, become women. It would appear, then, that every female human being is not necessarily a woman; to be so considered she must share in that mysterious and threatened reality known as femininity. Is this attribute something secreted by the ovaries? Or is it a platonic essence, a product of the philosophic imagination.[7]

She lent great force to the women's Liberation Movement in the mid-nineteenth century by laying bare the gross inequalities in society. Drawing heavily on disciplines like biology, psychology and history, she discusses girl's education, love, sex, marriage, prostitution and domestic drudgery as well. She frankly talks about sexual exploitation and sexual pleasure for women, and does not give way to sentiments while discussing "maternity."

The feminist movement was sparked off by Betty Friedan's book *The Feminine Mystique*, published in 1963. She interviewed many wives and mothers and discovered the falsity of a woman's achieving happiness and contentment in marriage and motherhood although they had been blessed with all the comforts of life. All were merely trying to seek fulfilment by playing the role of a devoted wife and caring mother. Friedan writes:

> For a woman, as for a man the need for self-fulfilment—autonomy, self-realisation, independence, individuality, self-actualisation—is as important as the sexual need, with as serious consequences when it is thwarted. Women's sexual problems are, in this sense, by-products of the suppression of her basic need to grow and fulfil her potentialities as a human being, potentialities which the mystique of feminism fulfilment ignores.[8]

Kate Millett is another important feminist of the twentieth century. Her book *Sexual Politics*, published in 1969, vehemently argues that the women are in such an intolerable, subordinate position in the patriarchal social setup that most of them repress and deny its existence. In the two studies conducted by her she found that, were the female children given a choice, most of them would prefer to be born a boy. She graphically explains the sense of insecurity in women and the problem society would face in future in the form of female foeticide through pre-natal sex-determination tests. She writes:

> The phenomenon of parents' prenatal preferences for male issues is too common to require such elaboration. In the light of the imminent possibility of parents actually choosing the sex of their child, such a tendency is becoming the cause of some concern in scientific circles.[9]

Germaine Greer, too, belongs to the same brand of militant feminism, and goes to the extent of saying that "if women are to affect a significant amelioration in their condition it seems obvious that they must refuse to marry."[10]

A few feminist writers also made their contribution to the women's movement. Sylvia Plath's *Bell Jar* is about Esther, a young innocent and oppressed heroine who later becomes vengeful. Sylvia uses the metaphor of an exquisitely handcrafted mat made by Mrs Willard for Esther's oppressive state. The mat is not a thing for interior decoration but is used to be soiled under feet. Esther thinks:

> And I know that in spite of all the roses and kisses and restaurant dinners a man showered on a woman before he married her, what he secretly wanted when the wedding

service ended was for her to flatten out under his feet like Mrs Willard's kitchen mat.[11]

Margaret Drabble, Doris Lessing, Iris Murdoch, Marilyn French and Margaret Atwood have also contributed greatly in the movement, and have been internationally acclaimed as great feminist novelists. A couple of centuries back women writers dare not express themselves honestly by defying the rigid norms laid down by society, inviting social censure. However, there were many spinster writers like Jane Austen, Emily Bronte, Stevie Smith, Charlotte Mew, Mananne Moor and Elizabeth Smith. But the freedom to express themselves from the core of their heart was sought at the price of giving up the so-called "Womanliness"—sex, marriage, children and the social status of a wife.

Now the times have changed for the better for women. Women writers today have a relatively greater measure of freedom and are venturing into regions of experience which were earlier considered taboo. Although a very conservative nation, India too has uninhibited women writers like Shobha De, who is a commercial success in pornography. However, in the West the women writers are relatively more militant feminists than their Indian counterparts.

In India, the Trio—Mulk Raj Anand, R.K. Narayan and Raja Rao—did not pay much attention to women emancipation. Although they had in their hand a great material on freedom movement and the role women played, they let themselves miss out on this opportunity. Excepting *The Old Woman and the Cow*, Anand is deeply involved in championing the cause of the have-nots. Gauri, its heroine, is a fine example of his idea of women's emancipation. Narayan's portrayal of women characters ranges from the meek and submissive wife of Margayya in *The Financial Expert* and Savitri in *The Dark Room* to the vibrant and radical women characters like Daisy and Rosie in *The Painter of Signs* and *The Guide* respectively. But Daisy and Rosie are not examples to be emulated, and Anand obliquely warns us of the destructive repercussions 'feminism' will have on society.

Women in Raja Rao's novels suffer from domestic injustice and tyrannical tradition, but the writer suggests no way out of their dilemma. His women characters, who are a little ambitious, end up playing the devoted role of a wife like Savitri in *The Serpent and the Rope*. Indian culture being rooted into his consciousness fails him to offer any concrete solution to the besetting women's issue.

Bhabani Bhattacharya's portrayal of women is too optimistic to be realistic. His women are tender, charming, and virtuous, and play a significant role in effecting social change. But in spite of being tender and virtuous, they are victimized. Kajoli in *So Many Hungers!* undergoes immense suffering and misery, but her spirit remains invincible. Mohini in *Music for Mohini* effects social reforms in Behula village steeped in superstitions and obsolete customs.

Thus, male writers, owing to a misconception about or ignorance of the women in general, have failed to give an honest or real portrayal of their women characters. They have either exposed their weaknesses and drawbacks, or placed her on a high pedestal and deified it. Thus, the delineation of the real woman has escaped the pen of male writers somehow. Kamala Markandaya's works are a realistic delineation of the double pulls that the Indian women is subjected to, between her desire to assert herself as an individual and her duty in the capacity of a daughter, wife and mother. She also points out how the socio-economic conditions affect the women most. Markandaya's first novel *Nectar in a Sieve* is a well-constructed novel on the classical model on the theme of hunger and starvation. As a tour de force on the peasant's life, their toil, their anguish, their misery and above all their tragedy, it has been justly compared with Pearl S. Buck's *The Good Earth*, Alan Paton's *Cry the Beloved Country* and K.S. Venkataramani's *Murugan the Tiller*. Rukmini, the narrator-protagonist, narrates in the reminiscent mode about the decline of her family into poverty. The socio-economic conditions affect Rukmini and her daughter Ira most. She experiences one misery after another. Her husband becomes unfaithful and even her daughter, Ira, resorts to prostitution to save the family from starvation. Markandaya, gives a vivid description of the social customs and traditions and shows how these add to the sufferings of women. Parents arrange marriages, and the size of dowry decides the status of the bridegroom.

Rukmini's elder sister was married off with suitable dowry, but Rukmini is married off to a tenant farmer for want of a suitable dowry.

Barren, childless women, especially those who fail to give birth to a son, are contemptuously looked down upon. A son carries on the name of the family from generation to generation. In the novel, Nathan wants a son and Rukmini gets a number of sons through the help of Dr Kenny. Thus, the disintegration of their marriage is averted. Ira is abandoned by her husband as she remains childless even after five years of her marriage, and by the time she gets medically cured of barrenness, her husband has taken another wife. Furthermore, Markandaya shows how a woman can attain a deeper self-knowledge, not through alienation and self-laceration but through expansion and communion. The novelist shows that within the traditional role, she can accommodate her other roles as a human being.

Her second novel, *Some Inner Fury,* is about Mirabai who is forced to part from her lover Richard in the heat of Quit India Movement. Besides, the novel is also about Premala who, finding her husband's home and his English friends disgusting, tries to seek relief by helping Hickey, an English missionary, to run a school for the village boys. She dies of suffocation when the school is set on fire. *Some Inner Fury* has been compared with Venkataramani's *Kandan, the Patriot.* Whereas Venkataramani is poetical and masculine, Markandaya is suggestive and feminist. In a *Silence of Desire*, the protagonist Sarojini overcomes her problems in her own way. Dandekar, after fifteen years of married life, begins to irritate with his god-fearing and religious wife. His wife's visits to a Swami for the cure of her tumour develops in him an inferiority complex. He becomes extremely meddlesome and possessive, but the more he tries to deviate her from the influence of the Swami, the more he fails. But finally all is well when the Swami leaves the city after advising Sarojini to undergo an operation for her tumour. Here Markandaya realistically portrays the complexity of man-woman relationship. In most of her novels women have been shown as a source of great latent strength that saves the male protagonists from collapse.

Ruth Prawer Jhabvala's novels are articulation of her own bitter experiences in an alien land. Preoccupied with the travails of the white woman in India, her delineation of the Indian women becomes limited and narrow, which only leaves the impression of being contemptible, flighty and pathetic. Hers is a feminine contemporary urban sensibility. Living in Delhi in the years after independence, Mrs Jhabvala has had opportunities of exercising her prowess of close observation on a milieu that changes like a chameleon. She has written prolifically and with versatility about personal relationships, man-woman relationships and domestic life. Her novels are: *To Whom She Will* (1955), *The Nature of Passion* (1956), *Esmond in India* (1958), *The Householder* (1960), *Get Ready for Battle* (1962), *A Backward Place* (1965), *A New Dominion* (1972) and *Heat and Dust* (1975).

To Whom She Will is a simple love story which presents vividly the modern Indian domestic life. It is a story in which love loses to tradition and family. Amrit is a dashing girl who submits to tradition. Jhabvala's first three novels are about both wife hunting and husband hunting. In her later novels she concentrates on the trapped married couple who seek a better mutual understanding, as in *The Householder* and in *A Backward Place*, or separation of the couple as in *Get Ready for Battle*.

Anita Desai's famous novels are *Cry the Peacock* (1963), *Voices in the City* (1965), *Bye Bye Blackbird* (1971), *Where Shall We Go This Summer?* (1975), *Fire on the Mountain* (1977), *Clear Light of Day* (1980) and *The Village by the Sea* (1982). The novelist has graphically presented the turbulent psyche of the modern Indian women. Her protagonists are intelligent, sensible and sensitive, but in an attempt to manage home and children and attain emotional fulfilment, they reach on the verge of mental crisis. Unable to cope with their crisis, they resort to drastic steps. Maya in *Cry, the Peacock*, kills her husband Gautama by pushing him from the roof. In *Where Shall We Go This Summer?*, the author lays bare the void in Sita's life as a woman, wife and mother. It is a poignant tale of a middle-aged woman torn between her desire to abandon her comfortable, albeit boring existence, and the realization that the bonds that bind her to it cannot easily be severed. Desai has been labeled as a great feminist writer of international acclaim for having presented the predicament of sensitive women characters trapped between tradition and modernity. She, however, does not suggest solutions to their problems.

Attia Hussain's famous novel *Sunlight on a Broken Column* (1961) created an indelible stamp on the readers' psyche. Written in a strictly autobiographical and retrospective mode, its plot deals with Laila's revolt against the joint family system. Although she lives a secure and sheltered life in a Muslim family with a Western outlook, she is denied the freedom that women in the West enjoy. The reins of the household are in the hands of Baba Jan, a dying grandfather and domineering patriarch. With the passage of time, the old order fast changes. Laila questions and rebels against the traditional values, and finally decides to marry Ameer, a man after her heart. In spite of the disapproval of the entire joint family, she marries Ameer. He joins the Army in 1942, is taken prisoner and gets killed while trying to escape. She has a daughter by him and learns to struggle and come to terms with life.

Attia Hussain's graphic description of scenes of college life, garden parties and receptions are vivid and informing. Her sharp and pointed remarks on social facts and orthodox conventions that enslave a woman, especially a Muslim one, earn for her a secure niche in the field of feminist writing in Indian English literature.

Nayantara Sahgal, yet another prominent Indian woman writer, dealt with issues concerning women that later became major issues in the feminist movement launched in the sixties. With delicate sensitivity, she exposes the prejudices women face in a male-dominated society. *The Day in Shadow* is about the prejudice faced by the divorcee-heroine Simrit. Sahgal, being a divorcee herself, reveals in a realistic and vivid manner how Simrit tries to square her equation with her growing children and her ex-husband. She not only undergoes the humiliation of being a divorcee but also faces the cruel "consent terms" of the divorce. Her best novel *Rich Like Us* is about Sonali, the daughter of a Marathi and a Kashmiri mother. Sonali, the central character, differs from the stereotypes of Indian womanhood found in fiction. She is a very brilliant IAS officer. She goes to Oxford to escape the Indian world of arranged marriages. She inherits from her father his uncompromising idealism and on her refusal to pass the sanction for the Happyola factory for Dev, she is replaced by the pliant Kachru. Besides, the emotional and mental trauma of Mona and Rose caused by their husband Ram is also vividly laid bare. Conditioned to the oppressive Indian social setup both become willing victims of exploitation and injustice. Sahgal has a limited world of feminist ideas. She does a close and sensitive study of her élite women characters. Her protagonists refuse to remain fettered to their subordinate roles and defy traditional norms and values in search of emancipation. Parallel to the main theme of man-woman relationships, runs the allegory of the impersonal world of the post-Nehru Indian political world.

Kamala Das, the renowned poetess, has written two novels: *The Alphabet of Lust* (1980) and *A Doll for the Child Prostitute*. They are about the quest for identity in a male-dominated society. The protagonists let themselves exploited sexually in their assertion for emancipation and search for identity. Even her autobiography *My Story* reveals her struggle for emancipation and search for identity.

Written in the autobiographical mode, *The Alphabet of Lust* is about Manasi, the unhappy and frustrated wife of a government official, Amol Mitra, who is old enough to be his father. The two are not suited to each other. All the time he is busy with his official work, and denies her love, companionship and warmth. In a state of frustration, despondency and diminished status, she hungers for emancipation and identity. She is so overwhelmed by her circumstances that she discards all barriers, inhibitions, whether moral or social. Using her political contacts she is able to become a poetess with a number of awards to her credit. She finally succeeds to become the Home Minister. By asserting her individuality unscrupulously, she soars to the highest pinnacle of success, power and glory.

A Doll for the Child Prostitute, her next novel, is about a child prostitute's struggle for liberation and quest for identity. To this end Mira, the child prostitute, secretly marries her student-client which doesn't last a week, and is forced back into the abhorrent profession of prostitution. Another child prostitute, Rukmini, too has similar pursuits. Her mother sells her to a brothel keeper and her craving to become a cultured and cultivated woman are frustrated. One Inspector Sahab, fond of her, wants to make her his "keep." She ironically begins to call her "Papa" as he resembles her father. Forgetting all his lust, he begins to behave as one. He had promised to bring a foreign doll for her and he makes good his promise. His carnal lust is changed into parental love and affection for her. The brothel keeper proposes to marry Rukmini to her son. Thus she gets an opportunity to identity herself as a decent and self-respecting woman. Thus, Kamala Das's novels are clear manifestations of a woman's quest for identity.

Namita Gokhale too has had her contribution to feminist writing written in the autobiographical mode. Her novel *Paro: Dreams of Passion* is about Paro's rebellion and her rejection of the culturally imposed sexual repression. All her inhibitions and moral barriers come to an end, and she becomes a nymphomaniac in search of sexual variety. In the character of Paro, sex is symbolic of a quest for identity as a free woman. Her sexual exploits are an expression of the free woman—the symbol and prototype of emancipation and individuality.

Shashi Deshpande holds great worth as an Indian English woman novelist. She is the only Indian author to have made bold attempts at giving a voice to the disappointments and frustrations of women despite her vehement denial of being a feminist. *Roots and Shadows*, her first novel, depicts the agony and suffocation experienced by the protagonist Indu in a male-dominated and tradition-bound society. She undergoes great mental trauma when she refuses to play the straitjacketed role of a wife imposed upon by society. The man she marries after her heart, to her great disappointment, is no different from the less educated and conservative Indian men. She is even more pained to realize that she herself has all along been unconsciously aping the role of the ideal Indian wife. In her quest for identity, she even develops an extra-marital affair to finally realize that it is possible to exercise autonomy within the parameters of marriage. Shashi Deshpande thus exposes the gross gender discrimination and its fallout in a male-dominated society.

The Dark Holds No Terrors, the second novel, is about the traumatic experience the protagonist Saru undergoes as her husband refuses to play a second-fiddle role. Saru undergoes great humiliation and neglect as a child and, after marriage, as a wife. Deshpande discusses the blatant gender discrimination shown by parents towards their daughters and their desire to have a male child. After her marriage, as she gains a greater social status than her husband Manohar's, all begins to fall apart. His husband's sense of inferiority complex and the humiliation he feels as a result of society's reaction to Saru's superior position develops sadism in him. Manu vents his frustration on Saru in the form of sexual sadism, which has been vividly portrayed by Deshpande.

That Long Silence, the third novel, is about Jaya who, despite having played the role of a wife and mother to perfection, finds herself lonely and estranged. Jaya realizes that she has been unjust to herself and her career as a writer, as she is afraid of inviting any displeasure from her husband. Her fear even discourages her from acknowledging her friendship with another man.

The Binding Vine, her fourth novel, deals with the personal tragedy of the protagonist Urmi to focus attention on victims like Kalpana and Mira. Urmi narrates the pathetic tale of Mira, her mother-in-law, who is a victim of marital rape in marriage. Mira, in the solitude of her unhappy marriage, would write poems, which were posthumously translated and published by Urmi. Urmi also narrates the tale of her acquaintance Shakutai, who had been deserted by her husband for another woman. The worst part of her tale is that her elder daughter Kalpana is brutally raped by her sister Sulu's husband, Prabhakar. Urmi takes up cudgels on Kalpana's behalf and brings the culprit to book.

In *A Matter of Time*, her fifth novel, Shashi Deshpande for the first time enters into the metaphysical world of philosophy. Basically, it's about three women from three generations from the same family and how they cope with the tragedies in their lives. Sumi is deserted by her husband Gopal, and she faces her humiliation with great courage and stoicism. Though, deep inside, she is struck with immense grief, but tries to keep herself composed for the sake of her daughters. Her mother Kalyani was married off to her maternal uncle Shripati. When their four-year-old son gets lost at a railway station,

Shripati sends her back to her parent's house. On Manorama's request, when he returns he maintains a stony silence for the rest of his life. Kalyani's mother Manorama fails to beget a male heir to her husband, and fears lest he should take another wife for the same purpose. Manorama, to avoid the property getting passed on to other family, gets Kalyani married to her brother Shripati. Thus, Deshpande has revealed to our gaze the fears, frustrations and compulsions of three women from three generations from the same family.

Small Remedies, her latest novel, is about Savitribai Indorekar, the aging doyenne of Hindustani music, who avoids marriage and a home to pursue her genius. She has led the most unconventional of lives, and undergoes great mental trauma due to the opposition by a society that practises double standards—one for men and the other for women. Even as a child she was a victim of gross gender discrimination. Besides, Madhu narrates her own life story and also those of her aunt Leela and Savitribai's daughter, Munni.

A deep analysis of her novels leaves no doubt about her genuine concern for women. Her protagonists are acutely aware of their smothered and fettered existence in an orthodox male-dominated society. Caught between tradition and modernity, her protagonists search for their identity within marriage. Deshpande's novels contain much that is feminist. The realistic delineation of women as wife, mother and daughter, their search for identity and sexuality as well, leaves the readers in no doubt where her real sympathies lie.

She has been against her works being labeled as "feminist," as it has traditionally been regarded as an inferior type of literature in the minds of people. She denies any influence of the militant kind that Western feminists like Simone de Beauvoir, Germaine Greer, Betty Friedan, and Kate Millett advocate. She concerns herself with the women's issues in the Indian context. In an interview she tells Lakshmi Holmstrom:

> It is difficult to apply Kate Millett or Simone de Beauvoir or whoever to the reality of our daily lives in India. And then there are such terrible misconceptions about feminism by people here. They often think it is about burning bras and walking out on your husband, children

or about not being married, not having children etc. I always try to make the point now about what feminism is not, and to say that we have to discover what it is in our own lives, our experiences.[12]

Women-centred narratives in her novels have led many interviewers to ask her as to what extent does she consider herself a feminist. Shashi Deshpande says:

> I now have no doubts at all in saying that I am a feminist. In my own life, I mean. But not consciously, as a novelist. I must also say that my feminism has come to me very slowly, very gradually, and mainly out of my own thinking and experiences and feelings. I started writing first and only then discovered my feminism. And it was much later that I actually read books about it.[13]

NOTES AND REFERENCES

1. *Hunter College Women's Studies Collective: Women's Realities, Women's Choices: Introduction to Women's Studies*, New Delhi: Oxford University Press, 1983, 68.

2. Quoted in Sarbjit K. Sandhu, *The Image of Woman in the Novels of Shashi Deshpande*, New Delhi: Prestige Books, 1991, 8.

3. Ramchandra Guha, "Not by Faith Alone," *The Sunday Express*, 1 October 1918.

4. K.S. Ramamurti, *Rise of the Indian Novel in English*, New Delhi: Sterling, 1987, 66.

5. John B. Alphonso-Karkala, *Indo-English Literature in the Nineteenth Century*, Mysore: University of Mysore, 1870, 78.

6. Sushila Singh, "Preface," *Feminism and Recent Fiction in English*, New Delhi: Prestige Books, 1991, 7.

7. Simone de Beauvoir, "Introduction," *The Second Sex*, translated and edited by H.M. Parshley, Harmondsworth: Penguin, 1983, 13.

8. Betty Friedan, *The Feminine Mystique*, Harmondsworth: Penguin, 1971, 282.

9. Kate Millett, *Sexual Politics*, London: Rupert Hart Davis, 1971, 56-57.

10. Germaine Greer, *The Female Eunuch*, St Alabama: Paladin, 1976, 319.

11. Sylvia Plath, *The Bell Jar*, London: Faber & Faber, 1982, 88-89.

12. Shashi Deshpande, "Interview: Shashi Deshpande Talks to Lakshmi Holmstrom," *Wasafiri*, No. 17, Spring 1993, 26.

13. *Loc. cit.*

2

ROOTS AND SHADOWS

—————◆—————

Roots and Shadows[1], Shashi Deshpande's first full length novel, is about the struggle of the protagonist Indu—representative of the educated, middle-class women—as to how her assertion of her individuality to achieve freedom leads to her confrontation with her family and the male-dominated society. Feeling smothered in an oppressive male-dominated and tradition-bound society, she attempts to explore her inner self to assert her individuality.

Indu returns to her ancestral home after a gap of eleven years, which is occasioned by her cousin Mini's marriage being performed in the traditional mode in their ancestral home. She leaves home at the age of eighteen to marry the man she loves. She returns on being summoned by *Akka*, the domineering matriarch, as she is on her deathbed. *Akka* has made her the sole heiress to her property, and the household atmosphere becomes charged with resentment by the family members for being excluded from the will. Deshpande presents with vivid details a large Maharashtrian Brahmin household, and the myriad women characters, their greed, jealousy, hopes, fears, disappointments, and their anguish.

Among the myriad women characters the old tyrannical matriarch *Akka* is worth special mention. She is rich and childless, and decides to stay in her brother's house after her husband's death. She wields absolute control over her brother's household, and her venomous tongue reduces Indu's grandfather *Kaka* into a tongue-tied, submissive character.

Akka representative of the old order, is so obsessed with untouchability that she refuses to move into a hospital for fear of getting polluted by the touch of nurses belonging to

other castes. She is also very particular about how a girl
should conduct herself in society, and reprimands Indu for
talking to a boy in the library. She is also dead against the
idea of Naren's mother wanting to learn music. She says:

> What learn music from a strange man! Sit and sing in
> front of strangers! Like THOSE women? Are we that kind
> of family? Isn't it enough for you to sing one or two
> devotional songs, one or two *aarti* songs? What more
> does a girl from a decent family need to know? (55).

Only after her death does Indu come to know about
Akka's life from Narmada *Atya*. *Akka* was married at twelve
and her husband—tall, bulky with coarse features—was well
past thirty. On the contrary *Akka* was small, dainty, pretty
with a round face, fair skin, straight nose and curly hair. She
went to her husband's house after six months. By the time
she was thirteen, she made two abortive attempts to run
away. Her mother-in-law whipped her and kept her starved
by locking her up in a room for three days. Then she was
sent to her husband's room. She cried and clung to her
mother-in-law saying, "Lock me up again, lock me up" (77).
But as *Akka* told Narmada that there was no escape from a
husband then. She even tells Narmada before the
consummation of her marriage: "Now your punishment begins
Narmada. You have to pay for all those saris and jewels" (77).

For child brides in those days, sex was a kind of punishment
against which they could do nothing and continued to suffer
in silence. Tara Ali Baig aptly observes: "Arch traditionalists
that women are it is they who have successfully and brutally
established man's ascendancy over women in society."[2] Thus,
Deshpande, unlike a militant feminist does not put the blame
squarely on man's shoulders, but reveals the contradictions
in a woman's character also.

The other side of *Akka*'s character is manifest in the way
she controls her husband after he is struck by total paralysis.
Although she takes excellent care of her paralyzed husband
for two years, but avenges herself of all that she had to
forbear (undergo) by not allowing his mistress, whom he
adores, to meet him. Her sadistic nature is also manifest
when *Akka* tells Narmada with a vicious pleasure that she

threw his mistress out when she had come to meet him. Narmada tells Indu that later that night she finds *Akka* in tears who tells her that after marriage no night passed without tears. Thus, Deshpande makes a strong statement on the arranged marriages, which are outright discriminatory towards women. A husband can have a mistress with impunity for his physical and mental needs, whereas a wife cannot take another man—her act is branded adultery. Neena Arora aptly remarks: "This condemnation is dictated by man's interest in preserving his property rather than by any moral consideration."[3]

Although *Akka* has undergone great suffering at her husband's house, on her return to her father's house after her husband's death, she enforces a rigid code of conduct on women in the household. She insists that a woman should never utter her husband's name, for it means not only disrespect towards him but also shortens his life span. But Indu, an educated upper middle-class woman, resents as to what connection there was "between a man's longevity and his wife's calling him by name? It's as bad as praying to the *tulsi* to increase his life span" (35).

But caught in the matrix of age-old custom or tradition, like the other Deshpande's women characters she cannot break herself free from the clutches of tradition. She painfully realizes that despite her education and exposure, she was no different from the women that circumambulated the *tulsi* plant to increase their husbands' life span. Even her husband who is educated and apparently a modern man, is only a typical Indian husband for whom she has to remain passive and submissive.

Several instances prove that all along Indu has been playing the role of wife to perfection to keep Jayant happy and satisfied. Despite her reluctance, she has to continue the frustrating job of writing for the magazine just to keep Jayant satisfied. She is against working for the magazine as she gets disillusioned by her experience with a so-called social worker, who had received an award for social services. Indu was so much impressed by that "soft spoken, [...] seemingly sincere and dedicated"(18) woman that she wrote an article on her. But then she is shocked after reading an article she received on that woman, as she realizes that it was "a story of shameless exploitation of ignorance, poverty and need. A story of ruthlessness and unscrupulousness in the pursuit of fame, power and money, all of which had come now" (18). When she shows the two stories about the same woman to her worldly-wise editor, he rejects the later story knowing full well that it was true. Appalled by the woman's hypocrisy and the editor's attitude, she tells Jayant about it who, steeped in his middle-class values merely says: "That's life! What can one person do against the whole system! No point making yourself ridiculous with futile gestures. We need the money, don't we? Don't forget we have a long way to go" (19). Thus, she continues to write what suits the magazine and not her own conscience. Gradually, but surely, she realizes the absurdity of the existence, as she has to compromise against her conscience with the values of a hypocrite society where success is counted sweetest. But all this was not to go for long. Circumstances bring her to the proverbial crossroads where every individual has to do some introspection sooner or later. Had *Akka*, her old domineering matriarch not called her, she wouldn't have had time enough to think about her identity and selfhood, which she had effaced just to prove that her marriage was a success. But her belated realization is manifest in her private conversation with Naren where she bares all. It was the height of hypocrisy she practises just to flaunt that Jayant and she belonged to the smart young set. She tells:

> We are rational, unprejudiced, broad-minded. We discuss.
> We discuss intelligently, even solemnly, the problems of unemployment, poverty, corruption and family planning.
> We scorn the corrupt. We despise the ignorant, we hate the wicked—and our hearts bleed, Naren for Vietnam, for the blacks, for the Harijans—but frankly we don't care a damn not one goddamn about anything but our own precious selves, our own precious walled-in-lives (28).

Indu, who had considered herself smart, educated, independent and clever, comes to the painful conclusion that she was no better than her *Kakis* and *Atyas*.

Several other incidents in the novel prove Indu's poignant awareness of the inequality Indian women had to reconcile with under compulsion. The drudgery of performing the countless household chores makes their life miserable and when this goes unrecognized, it makes then the more miserable. Indu is disgusted at the sight of strewn plates and littered remnants lying about after the meal. She becomes conscious of the exemplary patience and courage women have shown to clear up the mess after every meal. "And women like *Kaki* even ate off the same dirty plate their husbands had eaten in earlier. Martyrs, heroines, or just stupid fools" (73). Indu, calls the household chores tiresome, boring and frustrating like the job of Sisyphus. Simone de Beauvoir says:

> Few tasks are more like the torture of Sisyphus than housework, with its endless repetition; the clean becomes soiled, the soiled is made clean, over and over, day after day. The housewife wears herself out marking time. She makes nothing, simply perpetuates the present.[4]

She had become aware of the prevailing injustice in society since her childhood. No effort was spared to indoctrinate her to play the role of a meek and submissive daughter, wife, and mother. She tells Naren: "As a child they had told me I must be obedient and unquestioning. As a girl they had told me I must be meek and submissive," because "you are a female. It is the only way for a female to live and survive" (174). Even her womanhood is thrust upon her brutally and gracelessly, when she is told, "You're a woman now... You can have babies yourself" (87). She begins to hate herself as "for four days now you are unclean. You can't touch anyone or anything" (87). That was how she had been introduced into the beautiful world of womanhood.

Simone de Beauvoir refers to this dramatic conflict that every girl at puberty has to undergo as "she cannot become 'grown up' without accepting her femininity; and she knows already that her sex condemns her to a mutilated and fixed existence, which she faces at this time under the form of impure sickness and a vague sense of guilt."[5] Indu is conscious of the secondary position women have been condemned to. She asks her *Kaka* in jest, "Can you imagine them sending up a cup of tea for me? Women and children should know their places" (53). The shaven-head of a widowed domestic help reminds her how a widow had to remain shaven-headed all life after her husband's death for fear of getting ostracized. Indu's *Kaka* was dead against this idea and the widowed *Atya* "was now a second class citizen in the kingdom of widows. The orthodox would not eat food cooked by her" (130).

She also becomes painfully aware of the fact that she is incomplete and certainly not different from the breed of women she had forgotten after leaving home. All the time she misses Jayant and wants him to be beside her. She feels miserable and incomplete in Jayant's absence. She feels incomplete in yet another sense as her own academic and economic success does not make any special impact on the other household women: "To get married to bear children to have sons and then grandchildren they were still for them the only success a woman could have" (128). She has come far enough in life in comparison to her *Kaki*s and *Atya*s but back home she becomes painfully aware of her unenviable plight, as her marriage has not put her in a class apart. In the process she has lost her own self, her identity and needs. Jayant who hates any display of passion on Indu's part denies her even the most basic sexual need in marriage. Even in the privacy of their bedrooms, she is not let to shed her inhibitions. She tells Naren: "Jayant, so passionate, so ready, sitting up suddenly and say, 'no, not now', when I had taken the initiative" (91). Being so snubbed by Jayant she feels humiliated and disillusioned. In a choked voice, she tells Naren: "When I'm like that he turns away from me. I've learnt my lesson now. And so I pretend. I'm passive. And unresponsive. I am still and dead" (92). So her lot is not much different from the other household women. Like them she too has become "still and dead."

She rebels to become complete and independent, but painfully realizes that she is neither of the two. Although she is excited to be back home after an absence of eleven years, but all the while she feels herself incomplete without Jayant by her side. She thinks, "This is my real sorrow. That I can never be complete in myself" (34). Here lies the rub. All along she had struggled against a system to achieve completeness in herself, which certainly is well nigh impossible. How can she imagine being totally free and independent without being complete in herself. The compulsive circumstances had made her as diminished and submissive as any other wife. She has even become obsessed with Jayant: "When I look into the mirror, I think of Jayant, when I undress I think of him. Have I become a fluid with no shape, no form of my own?" (54). So she is on her way to become an ideal woman, a woman who doesn't have an independent identity of her own: "A woman who sheds her 'I' who loses her identity in her husband's" (54). Pitting her against the woman of the older generation, Deshpande has very artistically juxtaposed two sets of Indian women. The one is representative of Narmada, Kamala *Kaki*, Sumitra *Kaki*, *Atya*, and Sunanda *Atya*; and the other by Indu. Indu's academic achievement, economic independence and her independent attitude mean nothing to the woman of older generation, as their only aim in life was "to get married, to bear children, to have sons and then grandchildren" (128). Indu, representative of the new generation with a rational temperament tries to follow her own conscience but fails miserably under combined pressure of the tradition-bound society and the fear born of stigma attached to such independent attitude and existence.

In Shashi Deshpande's *Roots and Shadows*, much critical controversy has been raised about the author's motives regarding the incestuous relation between Indu and her cousin, Naren. It is Naren to whom she tells every little detail of her married life. Naren who was so natural to her and the easy compatibility that develops between the two, makes her take the most daring step of surrendering herself to him not once but twice in the novel. She indulges in the act with much wild abandon and cherishes it later without any guilt consciousness. She thinks:

> I can go back and lie on my bed. I thought, and it will be like erasing the intervening period and what happened between Naren and me. But deliberately I went to my bed and began folding the covers. I don't need to erase anything I have done, I told myself in a fit of bravado (168).

She resolves not to disclose this to Jayant as she thinks it had nothing to do with him. This assertion of her self has sparked off contradictory remarks from the reviewers. P. Bhatnagar laments:

Indu's casual and matter-of-fact attitude to what she had done is shocking. Have our morals really gone so low that woman commit this sin for nothing, just to prove that they do not lack courage? Is this really representative of the modern Indian woman?[6]

Another critic, P. Ramamoorthy does not view Indu's adultery as something negative but as something stemming from the predicament of the compulsive circumstance woman like Indu find themselves in. To Indu it is an exercise of autonomy within marriage. He observes:

This sheds a brilliant light on Indu's awareness of her autonomy and her realization that she is a being, and not a dependent on Jayant. The novel gains its feminist stance in Indu's exploration into herself but it also moves beyond the boundaries of feminism into a perception of the very predicament of the human existence.[7]

A society wherein a man takes sexual liberties with impunity and a woman indulging in the same is looked upon with shock and horror and branded an adulteress and much a harlot or loose lady. Deshpande probably is trying to shake the readers out of their complacency by thrusting in their face the double standards being practised in a patriarchal social setup.

Deshpande also highlights the problems that middle-class families encounter in their search for suitable grooms for their daughters. The case in point is that of Padmini, where the parents get her married off in desperation, and the stoic resignation with which the girl accepts her lot is exemplary and commendable. Padmini's acceptance of a groom with "heavy, coarse features and crude mannerism" (13), makes her wonder whether woman had any other choice but to accept and submit unconditionally. She thinks: "The woman had no choice but to submit, to accept. And I had often wondered... have they been born without wills, or have their wills atrophied through a lifetime of disuse? And yet Mini, who had no choice either, had accepted the reality, the finality, with a grace and compose that spoke eloquently of that inner strength" (6). Like Padmini, for the other Indian girls also, it is marriage that matters and not the man. The search for a man is so difficult that parents become anxious and desperate and, at one nod from the man, settle the marriage. Indu wonders what the reasons could have been behind Padmini's acceptance of a man who was no match for her. Padmini's reply to Indu's question is reflective of the mental trauma most Indian girls of marriageable age undergo:

> You don't know what it has been like. Watching *Kaka* and Hemant and even Madhav *Kaka* running around after eligible men. And then sending the horoscope and having it come back with a message, it doesn't match? And if the horoscope matched there was the meeting to be arranged. And mother and *Atya* slogging in the kitchen the whole day. And all those people coming and staring and asking all kinds of questions. And if we heard they were old fashioned people, I would dress up in an old fashioned manner and they would say, 'She's not modern enough.' And if I dressed up well, they would say, "She's too fashionable for us. Or too short. Or too tall. Or too something." And *Kaka* trying to laugh and talk to those people, while his eyes looked so [...] anxious. And I, feeling like as if I had committed a great crime by being born a girl. So we would have to go through with it all over again. And finally if, everything was fine, there was the dowry (135).

Since arranged marriage is not a marriage of two souls, Deshpande raises the seminal issue of arranged marriage if it was any good. Indu reflects Deshpande's views that an arranged marriage was nothing "but two people brought together after cold-blooded bargaining to meet, mate and reproduce so that the generations might continue?" (3).

Here, the novelist exposes the hypocrisy and double standards prevalent in society. The easily available Naren is not considered a suitable match for their daughter; instead they pay a handsome dowry for one who has nothing but his family's social status. Shashi Deshpande does not make any sweeping anti-dowry statements but raises the issue subtly to be pondered over by the readers.

Indu's experiences teach her that one should listen to the voice of one's conscience and be faithful to it. Freedom within marriage is possible if one dares to do what one believes is right and tenaciously follow it. This alone can bring harmony and fulfilment in life.

Indu decides to go back to Jayant with the hope that she would do what she thinks correct and not be dishonest to her inner self. She reflects:

> Now I would go back and see that home could stand the scorching touch of honesty. Nevertheless I knew I would not tell Jayant about Naren and me (205).

Learning from her bitter experiences, she realizes how an emancipated woman should be. She takes the firm decision on how *Akka*'s wealth is to be put to use, knowing full well that the other relatives would feel greatly offended. She does not care to make good her promise to the dead Naren and decides to spend on Vithal's education. All this shows how mature and detached she has become as she does not care for the likes and dislikes of the living or dead, and follows her own conscience.

Thus, Shashi Deshpande suggests that the modern Indian women should learn to conquer their fears and assert themselves. The novel ends on a note of compromise which is quite representative of the basic Indian attitude. With the conviction of rationale and accountability she holds steadfast to her decisions in a tradition-bound household, which is proof enough of her individuality.

NOTES AND REFERENCES

1. Shashi Deshpande, *Roots and Shadows*, Madras: Sangam Books, 1983.

2. Quoted in Meera Shirwadkar, *Image of Woman in the Indo-Anglian Novel*, New Delhi: Sterling, 1979, 26.

3. Neena Arora, *Nayantara Sahgal and Doris Lessing: A Feminist Study in Comparison*, New Delhi: Prestige Books, 1991, 61.

4. Simone de Beauvoir, *The Second Sex*, translated and edited by H.M. Parshley, Harmondsworth: Penguin, 1983, 470.

5. *Ibid.*, 351.

6. P. Bhatnagar, "Indian Womanhood: Fight for Freedom in *Roots and Shadows*," *Indian Women Novelists*, edited by R.K. Dhawan, New Delhi: Prestige Books, 1991, Set I, Vol. 5, 129.

7. P. Ramamoorthy, "My Life is My Own: A Study of Shashi Deshpande's Women," *Feminism and Recent Fiction* in English, edited by Sushila Singh, New Delhi: Prestige Books, 1991, 124.

3

THE DARK HOLDS NO TERRORS

◆

The Dark Holds No Terrors,[1] Shashi Deshpande's second novel, is about Saru—an educated, economically independent, middle-class wife—who is made conscious of her gender as a child and whose loveless relationship with her parents and strained relations with her husband lead to her agonizing search for herself. The novel opens with Saru's return to her parents' house fifteen years after she left home with a vow never to return. Her relations with her husband become unbearably strained and she returns for some solace. Here she gets a chance to think over her relationships with her husband, her children, her parents and her dead brother, Dhruva.

Saru's relationship with her brother has been given special presentation. She is ignored in favour of her brother, Dhruva. No parental love is showered on her and she is not given any importance. Her brother's birthdays are celebrated with much fanfare and performance of religious rites, whereas her birthdays are not even acknowledged. She even feels that her birth was a horrible experience for her mother, as she later recalls her mother telling her that it had rained heavily the day she was born and it was terrible for her mother. It seemed to Saru that it was her birth that was terrible for her and not the rains.

She recalls the joyous excitement in the house on the occasion of his naming ceremony. The idea that she is a liability to her parents is deeply implanted in her mind as a child. Her mother's adoration of her son at her daughter's cost is the rallying point for the novelist to bring her feminist ideas together. The preference for boys over girls can be openly witnessed in most Indian homes, and is inextricably

linked to the Indian psyche. Sons bring in dowry could be
one reason, but the Indian society steeped in tradition and
superstition considers the birth of a son as auspicious as he
carries on the family lineage. The first thought that rose in
Saru's mind at hearing about her mother's death is: "Who lit
the pyre? She had no son to do that for her. Dhruva had been
seven when he died" (17). As Sarbjit Sandhu aptly remarks:

> The mother is very attached to her son. Her attitude is a
> typical one—after all, he is male child and therefore one
> who will propagate the family lineage. In another sense,
> also, the male child is considered more important than
> a girl, because he is qualified to give "agni" to his dead
> parents. The soul of the dead person would otherwise
> wander in ferment.[2]

Her mother constantly reminds her that she should not
go out in the sun as it would worsen her already dark
complexion. Saru recalls her conversation with her mother:

"Don't go out in the sun, you'll get darker."
"Who cares?
"We have to care if you don't. We have to get you
married."
"I don't want to get married."
"Will you live with us all your life?"
"Why not?"
"You can't."
"And Dhruva?"
"He's different. He's a boy" (40).

This sort of blatant discrimination between Saru and her
brother leads to a sense of insecurity and hatred towards her
parents, especially mother, and her resultant rebellious nature.
Y.S. Sunita Reddy observes: "In this connection, Saru's mother's
attitude is typical of most Indian mothers and a common
enough phenomenon in the Indian context."[3]

The turning point in her life is the accidental death of her
brother by drowning. All her life she is haunted by the
memories of her mother accusing her of intentionally letting
Dhruva die by drowning: "You did it, you did this, you killed
him" (173). She too on her part has a guilty conscience as
she considers herself responsible for having remained a mute

spectator to her brother's death by drowning. She never refutes the charge leveled against her by her mother. As G. Dominic Savio observes: "Dhruva's demise had always been her subconscious desire and there is a very thin demarcation between her wish and its fulfilment."[4] Shashi Deshpande thus reveals the social aspect of keen sibling jealousy born of a mother's undue fondness for the son.

Saru's mother's discriminatory behaviour makes Saru feel unloved and unwanted leading to a sense of alienation and estrangement. She is in the grips of insecurity. After her brother's death her lot deteriorated from bad to worse. Irrespective of geographical or chronological space, any Indian girl is a victim of gender discrimination in the Indian social setup. As S. Anandalakshmi opines: "The birth of a son gives a woman status and she invests herself in her son's fixture, creating a deep symbiotic bond."[5]

Saru's mother could be no exception to this and she loses interest in life after her son's death. She puts the blame for her own wretched lot squarely on Saru's shoulders. She snatches every opportunity to reproach her and takes no interest in education, career or future. Her feeling of being unwanted is so acute that she begins to hate her own existence as a girl or woman. On attaining puberty she says scornfully, "If you are a woman, I don't want to be one" (62). The treatment that is meted out to her during her monthly ordeals is inhuman. She is treated like an untouchable, segregated from the other members of the family and made to sleep on a straw mat with a cup and plate exclusively meant for her to be served in from a distance. She is engulfed with a sense of shame and prays in desperation for a miracle to put an end to it.

Thus, unloved and unwanted, she develops hatred towards the traditional practises during her impressionable years. Her hatred towards her mother is so acute that she becomes rebellious just to hurt her, "I hated her, I wanted to hurt her, wound her, make her suffer" (142). This hatred drives her to leave home for Bombay to seek medicine as a career. In the medical college she falls in love with a college mate and marries him against her parents' wishes. Her orthodox mother

was dead against her daughter's marrying a man from a
lower caste:

> "What caste is he?"
> "I don't know."
> "A Brahmin?"
> "Of course, not."
> Then cruelly... "His father keeps a cycle shop."
> "Oh, so they are low-caste people, are they?"
> The word her mother had used, with the disgust, hatred
> and prejudice of centuries had so enraged her that she
> had replied... "I hope so" (96).

Had her mother not been so against him, she would
probably not have married him and brought herself to such a
miserable condition. She later recollects:

> If you hadn't fought me so bitterly, if you hadn't been
> so against him, perhaps, I would never have married
> him. And I would not have been here, cringing from the
> sight of his hand-writing, hating him and yet pitying
> him too (96).

Devoid of love and security, she wanted to be loved.
When she gets attention from Manu, she wonders, "How could
I be anyone's beloved? I was the redundant, the unwanted,
an appendage one could do without" (66).

The need of the moment was a relation with someone
who could give her love and security. She thinks: "The
fisherman's daughter couldn't have been more surprised when
the king asked her to marry him than I was by Manu's love
for me" (66). Later when her relations become strained with
Manu she regrets for having rushed into marriage
unconditionally: "The fisherman's daughter was wiser. She
sent the king to her father and it was the father who bargained
with him, while I [...] I gave myself up unconditionally.
Unreservedly to him, to love him and to be loved" (66). The
circumstances that lead to her taking such a step, are the
making of her own parents. As Sunita Reddy opines: "If her
mother had provoked her by her blatant hostility, her father
had contributed to her present predicament by remaining a
mute spectator in the family drama."[6]

Saru considers herself the luckiest woman on earth, as the initial years of her marriage are sheer bliss. Manu is her saviour and the romantic hero who rescues Saru—a damsel in distress. She marries to secure the lost love in her parental home and her identity as an individual. As S.P. Swain writes: "Her marriage with Manu is an assertion on and affirmation of her feminine sensibility."[7] Although, Saru refrains from any physical indulgence with Manu but, after marriage, she revels in it with wild abandon:

> I became in an instant a physically aroused woman with an infinite capacity for loving and giving, with a passionate desire to be absorbed by the man I loved. All the cliches, I discovered were true, kisses were soft and unbearably sweet, embraces hard and passionate, hands caressing and tender, and loving, as well as being loved was an intense joy. It was as if little nerve ends of pleasure had sprung up all over my body (40).

Her dingy one-room apartment with "the corridors smelling of urine, the rooms with their dark sealed in odours" (40), is "a heaven on earth" for her. But soon all this proves to be a mere mirage for her. Soon she realizes that happiness is illusory. Saru remembers how a particular incident becomes a turning point in their blissful marital relationship. One night she returns home late in her bloodstained coat as she helped out the victims in a fire accident in a factory nearby. The neighbourhood thus comes to know about her identity, and she gains recognition. People would come to her for medical help and other related matters. In the beginning Saru could not realize the change that had come in Manu. Her success as a well-known and reputed doctor becomes the cause of her strained marital relations with Manu. In a retrospective mood she says much later: "He had been the young man and I his bride. Now I was the lady doctor and he was my husband" (42).

Manu is uncomfortable with Saru's steady rise in status, as he feels ignored when people greet and pay attention to Saru. Besides she is unable to spare time enough for Manu and children. Manu and Saru want to move out to some other place for their own reasons. While Manu feels humiliated and embarrassed, Saru is no longer happy in that cramped

and stinking apartment and wants to move into something
more decent. Earlier she was happy and contented to live on
Manu's salary but in her new role as career woman she
becomes discontented. She resents:

> For me, things now began to hurt. [...] a frayed saree I
> could not replace, a movie I could not see, an outing I
> could not join in. I knew now that without money life
> became petty and dreary. The thought of going on this
> way became unbearable (92).

Manu does not love her as he used to earlier. Saru begins
to hate this man-woman relationship, which is based on need
and attraction and not love. She scorns the word "love" now.
She realizes there was no such thing between man and woman.

With the change of circumstances she feels a gradual
disappearance of love and attachment towards husband and
children. The most solemn duties towards them remain
unattended to. The children are denied due love and care as
she gets late in the evenings.

While her social and financial status rises gradually, there
is an inverse decline in her conjugal relationship. Her relations
with Manu would have somehow moved on smoothly had
she remained contented with treating people in the
neighbourhood. But her ambition to move higher in life by
furthering her career through Boozie, who is a handsome and
efficient doctor. He is flirtatious in nature and Saru has no
aversion towards flirts. Their relation reaches a stage when
Boozie helps her financially to set up her own practice in a
posh area. Saru, blind in ambition, is unscrupulous in her
relationship with Boozie and consoles herself by treating it as
a mere teacher-student relation. She tells herself, "It was just
a teacher-student relationship. If he put his hand on my
shoulder, slapped me on my back, held my hand or hugged
me [...] that was just his mannerism and meant nothing. It
had nothing to do with me and Manu" (91). Both had their
own vested interests in sustaining such a relation. Boozie
openly flaunts his relationship with Saru to hide his
homosexual nature and Saru wanted to exploit him through
her feminine wiles to achieve her much coveted goal of
becoming an established, reputed doctor. Although there is

nothing physical about Saru-Boozie relationship, but this gives rise to a misconception in Manu's mind. But she had such a loathing towards Manu that she does nothing to placate him, rather lets him believe the obvious.

Even at the inauguration of her consulting room, when Boozie flaunts her by his side openly before the invitees to the programme, she feels resentful towards her husband:

> I could feel the stares. Everyone's except Manu's who would not look at us. And I should have hated him then. [...] not Manu, for he had done nothing then for which I could hate him, but this attractive, ravishingly masculine man who was doing this deliberately. Attracting attention to the two of us. But funnily enough, it was not him I hated, it was Manu for doing nothing (94).

But Saru's rise in social and financial status in contrast to Manu's status of an underpaid lecturer sets in great discomfort in their conjugal relation. Saru's contentment in her career is no match to her discontentment at home. And contrary to the claims of most feminists, she does not achieve fulfilment in life. Betty Friedan asserts: "For woman, as for man, the need for self-fulfilment—autonomy, self-realization, independence, individuality, self-actualization is as important as the sexual need, with as serious consequences, when it is thwarted."[8]

In a reminiscent mood she recalls one particular incident which leads to her loathing towards Manu. It was on the day when they had been watching a TV programme. She recalls:

> [Manu] had been sitting with his feet up on a stool, [...] soft, white, unmarked and flabby. Like his hands. And his laugh [...] it was rather silly. A kind of bray almost. Why had she never noticed that before? And had he always picked at his ears that way, deftly, rather stealthily? It was like seeing a man she had never seen, never seen, never known. [...] now that she knew him, she rather despised (135).

Certain incidents aggravate the already strained relation between the two to the extent that in the privacy of their room at night he doesn't behave like a husband, but a rapist. In an interview with Saru when the interviewing girl happens to ask Manu innocently: "How does it feel when your wife earns not only the butter but most of the bread as well?" (200). The three—Saru, Manu, and the girl—merely laughed it off as if it were nothing. This particular incident is very humiliating to him and he feels helpless and effeminate. To gain his masculinity he gives vent to his feelings through his beastly sexual assault on Saru. Although he is a cheerful normal human being and a loving husband during day, he turns into a rapist, to assert his manhood. In yet another incident she undergoes this nightmarish experience. Prior to going on a vacation to Ooty while shopping Manu and Saru happen to meet the former's college mate and his wife. During the talk Manu tells his colleague that they were going to Ooty. When his colleague expresses his inability and bad luck in affording such a vacation, the colleague's wife replies that he also could have afforded it had he married a doctor. A humiliated Manu once again victimizes Saru. She expresses her helplessness to her father: "I couldn't fight back. I couldn't shout or cry, I was so afraid the children in the next room would hear. I could do nothing. I can never do anything. I just endure" (201). Although she has achieved economic independence, her plight is miserable, as she has to perform double duties. Besides practicing medicine she has to fulfil the assigned job of a housewife. She expresses her desire to leave her medical practice but Manu dissuades her from doing so, as their standard of living wouldn't be possible on Manu's income.

The circumstances seem all the more intolerable as Manu feigns ignorance in the mornings of his beastly behaviour at night. At this juncture she comes to know about her mother's death. Despite her vow never to return home, she does so. She has reasons to do so as she won't have to undergo the humiliation of her mother's taunts, and she has an explanation to give to her father for her returning home on account of her mother's death.

At her father's house she objectively mulls over the reasons of her disastrous marriage. She blames herself for it as she easily identifies the consequences of the shattered male ego. The novel may be said to be a study in guilt consciousness, as Saru ruminates, "My brother died because I heedlessly turned my back on him. My mother died alone because I deserted her. My husband is a failure because I destroyed his manhood" (217). But what Shashi Deshpande suggests is the gender discrimination by parents towards their children, and the compulsion to perpetuate male dominance if the marriage is to be kept going. Thus, she has presented a realistic picture of the gross gender inequality prevailing in our society.

Although she returns to her parents' place in a detached frame of mind, she feels strange despite the fact that nothing had changed in the house, not even the seven pairs of large stone slabs leading to the front door on which she had played hopscotch as a child. Her father also sounds strange as he talked like an unwilling host to her as if she were an unwelcome guest. She is in grave need of sympathy but he does nothing to console her. This reminds her of the fate of a sister of her friend's who had come home after her disastrous marriage. She remembers how she received care and sympathy from her parents. Because her marriage had been an arranged one, the parents too were party to her misfortune. Since Saru's was not an arranged one, she makes herself solely responsible for her disastrous marriage and is guilty conscious. She is totally confused and feels that she has done great injustice towards her brother, mother, husband, and children.

On one occasion Saru presents a perfect recipe for a successful marriage. On being asked by her friend Nalu to talk on Medicine as a profession for women, to a group of college students, she says:

> A wife must always be a few feet behind her husband. If he is an MA, you should be a BA. If he is 5'4" tall you shouldn't be more than 5'3" tall. If he is earning five hundred rupees, you should never earn more than four hundred and ninety, if you want a happy marriage. Don't ever try to reverse the doctor-nurse, executive-secretary, principal-teacher role. It can be traumatic, disastrous. And I assure you, it is not worth it. He'll suffer. You'll suffer and so will the children. Women's magazines will tell you that a marriage must be an equal partnership. That's nonsense, rubbish. No partnership can ever be equal. It will always be unequal but take care that it's unequal in favour of your husband. If the scales tilt in your favour, god help you, both of you (137).

Retrospectively she also thinks about her relationship with Padmakar, her classmate in medical college, who she happens to meet years later. After a few meeting Saru dissuades him from attempting to forge a deeper relationship with her. She does so after realizing that such a relationship was no comfort. Now she had no illusions about romances or love for these two had lost relevance in her life: "Love? Romance? Both, I knew too well, were illusions and for me, sex was now a dirty word" (133). Through her relations with Boozie and Padmakar, she achieves no happiness and fulfilment. These extra-marital relations are no solace and compensation for her tense married life. Kamini Dinesh aptly remarks: "There cannot be an 'escape route', from the tension of married life. The woman seeking a crutch has, finally to fall back on herself."[9]

Shashi Deshpande contrasts Saru's life with the lives of her two school friends—Sunita and Nalu. Sunita leaves no effort to pose as a happily married woman. All the while she talks about her intimacy with her husband as if she were a non-entity without him, which only invokes pity in the eyes of the reader and hatred of her two friends. Nalu also questions her as to why she let her husband change her name from Sunita to Anju: "Do you have to surrender so easily?" (117). Nalu is contemptuous of Sunita's constant references to her husband and hates her for her submissive attitude of satisfying every whim of his. She tells her, "Well, I refuse to call you Anju or Gitanjali or whatever. To me you are Sunita and will always be Sunita" (118).

On the other hand is Nalu, a spinster who is a teacher and lives with her brother and his family. Saru contrasts Nalu with the Nalu of her college days who was full of enthusiasm. But now bitterness has crept into her, and Saru does not blame her bitterness on her spinsterhood. Saru feels that it would be wrong to say that Nalu "is bitter because she never married, never bore a child. But that would be as stupid as calling me fulfilled because I got married and I have borne two children" (121). Shashi Deshpande contrasts the lives of Saru, Sunita and Nalu and shows that a wife, a mother and a spinster had their own share of joys and sorrows, and it is almost difficult to conclude as to who is the more happier or the more fulfilled. While the married women are reported to be dissatisfied with their marriage, the unmarried ones are reported to have their own sufferings and anxieties. Betty Friedan observes: "Strangely a number of psychiatrists stated that, in their experience unmarried women patients were happier than married ones."[10]

A mature Saru now shuns extremes and takes a practical view of the circumstances. She is neither the typical Western liberated woman nor an orthodox Indian one. Shashi Deshpande does not let herself get overwhelmed by the Western feminism or its militant concept of emancipation. In quest for the wholeness of identity, she does not advocate separation from the spouse but a tactful assertion of one's identity within marriage.

NOTES AND REFERENCES

1. Shashi Deshpande, *The Dark Holds No Terrors*, New Delhi: Penguin, 1990.

2. Sarbjit K. Sandhu, *The Image of Woman in the Novels of Shashi Deshpande*, New Delhi: Prestige Books, 1991, 19-20.

3. Y.S. Sunita Reddy, *A Feminist Perspective on the Novels of Shashi Deshpande*, New Delhi: Prestige Books, 2001, 51.

4. G. Dominic Savio, "A Woman's Heritage of the Commonwealth: A Study of *The Dark Holds No Terrors*," *Women in the Novels of Shashi Deshpande*, ed. Suman Bala, New Delhi: Khosla Publishing House, 2001, 61.

5. S. Anandalakshmi, "The Female Child in a Family Setting," *The Indian Journal of Social Work*, Vol. LII, No. 1, January 1991, 31.

6. Y.S. Sunita Reddy, *op. cit.*, 56.

7. S.P. Swain, "Shashi Deshpande's *The Dark Holds No Terrors*: Saru's Feminine Sensibility," *Indian Women Novelists*, ed. R.K. Dhawan, New Delhi: Prestige Books, 1990, Set I, Vol. 4, 35-36.

8. Betty Friedan, *The Feminine Mystique*, Harmondsworth: Penguin, 1971, 282.

9. Kamini Dinesh, "Moving out of the Cloistered Self: Shashi Deshpande's Protagonists," *Margins of Erasure: Purdah in the Sub-continental Novel in English*, ed. Jasbir Jain and Amina Amin, New Delhi: Sterling, 1995, 200.

10. Betty Friedan, *op. cit.*, 23.

4

THAT LONG SILENCE

$\blacklozenge$

Shashi Deshpande's *That Long Silence*[1] is an expression of the silence of the modern Indian housewife. Although many women writers tried their hand at expressing this long silence that had turned woman into non-entities, they could only provide psychological depths to their characters. They either created unreal sentimental romances or finally succumbed to the temptation of mouthing feminist ideology. But Shashi Deshpande's success lies in her representation of real life experience. She realistically depicts the inner conflicts of Jaya and her quest for the self or identity. About *That Long Silence*, she says:

> And then I wrote *That Long Silence* almost entirely a woman's novel nevertheless, a book about the silencing of one-half of humanity. A lifetime of introspection went into this novel, the one closest to me personally; the thinking and ideas in this are closest to my own.[2]

Thus, Jaya represents half the humanity. The novel sustains its credibility from the fact that Jaya is a convent-educated English-speaking lady with a literary taste. It portrays the conflict raging between the narrator's split self—the writer and the housewife.

The novel opens with Jaya and her husband Mohan moving back into the old Dadar flat in Bombay from their cosy and palatial house. Her husband is involved in a financial malpractice and an inquiry against him is set up. Mohan is consoled to find that the children, Rahul and Rati, are away on a long tour with their family friends, and expects Jaya to go into hiding with him, which she refuses to comply with.

It is here in the small old Dadar flat that shorn of the usual domestic routine she becomes an introvert and goes into deep contemplation of her past and her childhood. Had there been no such crisis in their life, she would never have given a thought on herself or her individuality. Adele King opines: "Jaya finds her normal routine so disrupted that for the first time she can look at her life and attempt to decide who she really is."[3]

For seventeen long years of her marriage she successfully manages to suppress her feelings as she thought it more important to be a good wife than being a good writer. In her zeal to play out the role of a loyal wife and a caring mother, she has suppressed her desires that lead to self-actualization and fulfilment. She not only suppresses her writing career but also her association with her one-time neighbour, Kamat. Her career as a successful writer is jeopardized right in the early years of her marriage. A short story of hers bags the first prize and also gets published in a magazine. She is on the threshold of getting recognition as a creative writer of some merit, when Mohan expresses his displeasure at a particular story written by her. The story is about a man who cannot reach out to his wife except through her body. Mohan suspects if the man portrayed in the story is not he himself, and is apprehensive lest people should take him for the man in the story. She thinks, "Looking at his stricken face, I had been convinced I had done him wrong. And I had stopped writing after that" (144). But the writer in her goads her on to keep writing. She begins to write under a pseudonym, which doesn't help, and her stories are rejected one after another. Her neighbour Kamat, analyses the reasons behind the successive rejections and tells her that her stories lack strong emotions as she has suppressed her anger and frustration. But she cannot express her anger or feelings lest it should damage her relation with Mohan. She had learnt to control her anger, as Mohan considered this trait in a woman as "unwomanly" (83). She tells Kamat: "Because no woman can be angry. Have you ever heard of an angry young woman?" (147). At this Kamat warns her against indulging in self-pity as it would only prove destructive to her. He admonishes her: "Beware of this 'women are the victims' theory of yours. It will drag you down into a soft, squishy bog of self-pity. Take yourself seriously, women. Don't skulk behind a false name" (148). Later she begins to write light humorous pieces on the travails of a middle-class housewife in a column entitled "Seeta." She not only gets encouraging response from the readers but also a nod of approval from Mohan. Jaya says:

> Seeta had been the means through which I had shut the door firmly on all these women who had invaded my being, screaming for attention; women I had known I could not write about, because they might, it was just possible, resemble Mohan's mother or aunt or my mother or aunt (149).

Thus she had merely been glossing over the reality or truth, and smothering her inner conscience to avoid endangering her marriage. She denies her writings the reflections of her individuality or self to play the role model of a typical Indian middle-class woman. Kamat understands her literary capability and criticizes her for writing such stuff: "I can never imagine you writing this" (149). Adele King aptly observes: "In Jaya's stories they lived happily ever after although she knows the falsity of the view of life."[4]

Her association with Kamat, a widower living above her flat, lends yet another dimension to Jaya's personality. She is drawn towards him as he treats her as his equal, and offers constructive criticism to Jaya on her writings. He even receives her mail at his address to help her avoid any confrontation with her husband as he disapproves of her writings. He showers his attention on her, as he is lonely. Unlike other men he does not have aversion to cooking and such other domestic chores meant to be performed by women exclusively. She feels so much at ease in his company that her womanly inhibitions wither and she opens up her problems to him. He warns her against wallowing in self-pity and asks her to pursue her literary career by giving expression to her real inner self.

She becomes so uninhibitive towards Kamat that their relation leads to physical attraction. Sometimes his behaviour is father-like which on occasions turns into lover-like. The two are so much at ease in each other's company that he even makes personal remarks about her physical appearance. He says: "I prefer clean, spare lines in a human being. You, for example—your name is like your face" (152). On one occasion she even comes close to surrendering herself when she finds herself in his arms as he tries to console her at her remembrance of her father's death. In the seclusion of his apartment she had ample opportunity for physical indulgence but she dare not do so for fear of jeopardizing her marriage. It is yet again for this very reason that she feigns detachment towards his death, when on one of her visits to his apartment she finds him lying dead on the floor in his flat. She remains passive, as she does not want to endanger her marriage. The incident is proof enough of the fettered selves of so-called educated middle-class wives.

Besides these, there are many more reasons that deny the fulfilment of her individuality. In her zeal to play out the role of a loyal wife and a caring mother, she smothers her real self. Like the other women she has been indoctrinated right from her childhood. She does not protest the change of her name from Jaya to Suhasini at her marriage just to keep Mohan happy. Her dress and her appearance are proof of her submission to Mohan's liking, replicating an absorbed family-woman. She has systematically suppressed her free will as she has been taught "the importance and necessity of stable marriage and family—family as security, as a source of emotional strength."[5] But the same is denied to her. The crisis at Mohan's office begins to affect the affairs at home. She realizes that Mohan has lost interest in her. At the Dadar flat she has time to ponder over her relations with Mohan, and also to analyze and recognize her suppressed "self." Her emotional crisis comes to such a pass that she is afraid lest something should happen to Mohan. She cannot imagine a life without Mohan or his support:

> The thought of living without him had twisted my insides, his death had seemed to me the final catastrophe. The very idea of his dying had made me feel so bereft that tears had flowed effortlessly down my cheeks. If he had been a little late coming home, I had been sure he was dead. By the time he returned, I had, in my imagination shaped my life to a desolate widowhood (96-97).

Jaya's predicament is born of her split psyche. She represents the urban, middle-class woman who is educated and has had exposure to liberal Western ideas. Her upbringing demands the suppression of the self so the marriage can survive. Unable to free herself from the traditional code of conduct, her inner voice remains inarticulate even in her writings, and her pent-up feelings make her neurotic. The counsels of her aunts keep ringing in her ears, and this becomes the cause of her undoing. For instance, Vanita *Mami* counsels her just before her marriage: "Remember Jaya, a husband is like a sheltering tree. Keep the tree alive and flourishing, even if you have to water it with deceit and lies" (32). She further says: "If your husband has a mistress or two, ignore it. Take up a hobby instead, cats, may be, or your sister's children" (32). Although Jaya does not take Vanita *Mami*'s counsel seriously but for her part she does not prove herself different from her. When the occasion to choose between her family and husband arises, she chooses the former.

When the times are smooth, the relations between the two move on smoothly. But the crisis unmasks the two—Jaya and Mohan. Before the crisis, like her mythological counterpart Sita and Gandhari, she remains stuck to her husband and childrem. But after the crisis she is not willing to go into hiding with her husband. She is ashamed of the incident, and Mohan defends himself by saying, "It was for you and the children that I did this" (9). Mohan's trouble is his own making and he expects her to share this crisis unconditionally. Indira Bhatt observes that Mohan wants to "use his wife as buffer, an opiate to soften the impact of the forces he has set into motion against himself."[6]

She feels herself totally lost as she is taken for granted by Mohan. She realizes that her own feelings and emotions don't mean anything to him. Her realization that she is a non-entity in his eyes hurts her. In an earlier incidents when her paternal uncle Ramu *Kaka* shows her the family tree wherein even boys of the family find mention but her name is missing. She questions this patriarchal family tree at which he says: "How can you be here? You don't belong to this family. You have no place here" (142-43). Jaya is also shocked to find no mention of her mother, her aunts and even *Ajji* who kept the family together. She is full of anger and desperation over such gross gender discrimination.

Shashi Deshpande is very realistic in the sense that she suggests marriages are not based on love but convenience. Jaya is content to play the role of a caring wife as long as the economic and social conditions are fine. She happily plays out the role model of Gandhari:

> If Gandhari, who bandaged her eyes to become blind like her husband could be called an ideal wife, I was an ideal wife too. I bandaged my eyes tightly. I didn't want to know anything. It was enough for me that we moved to Bombay; that we could send Rahul and Rati to good schools, that I could have the things we needed—decent clothes, a fridge, a gas connection, travelling I class (61-62).

But unlike Sita, she fails to accompany her husband into exile. Mohan's heydays were over, and their marriage runs into rough weather. But she cannot be said to be wholly responsible, as Mohan too has his own share of responsibility. He wants to use Jaya as a cushion in this crisis. Jaya has changed much after her marriage. Her aunt's counsel, her father's advice—never to hurt Mohan—have made her bear things without opposition. Soon after marriage a quarrel between the two had led to Mohan's lapsing into silence altogether. She has a guilty conscience and begins to use silence stratagem to avoid any confrontation. The bubble of this long silence gets so bloated that this unexpected crisis bursts it. She had been lulled into silence till Mohan was a "sheltering tree." With his safe job and career, her home and children were safe. But the sudden inquiry against him makes her feel insecure. It's a tragedy that she herself needs somebody to console her that at last everything will be all right. Mohan accuses Jaya, and says: "Do you think I haven't seen how changed you are since we came here, since I told about my situation" (12). At this Jaya begins to laugh hysterically, and cannot help it. She herself doesn't know the cause. Mohan is so enraged that he leaves the house in a huff as if he would never return. She is left all alone and at this juncture she gets the news that Rahul has disappeared while holidaying. She feels totally shattered and lost, as there is nobody at hand to help her. She is in a traumatic state for many days, but finally everything is all right. Rahul is back and she also gets a telegram from Mohan that "All is well." Now she has come to terms with herself. During this period she articulates her long silence—her innermost thoughts, her fears, her doubts and all that she had suppressed during her seventeen years of marriage. While penning down her experiences, she undergoes a sort of catharsis. She has decided not to be passive and silent. She says:

> The panic has gone, I am Mohan's wife. I had thought, and cut off the bits of me that had refused to be Mohan's wife. Now I know that kind of a fragmentation is not possible (191).

Shashi Deshpande's canvas abounds in women characters as victims of the gross gender inequality. Mohan's mother and his sister Vimla too are such victims. His mother made a living by cooking for wedding feasts. Mohan's father was a drunkard who would frequently beat her up. Mohan narrates to Jaya a poignant incident when his father returned home late one night and found that *chutney* had not been served with rice to him. He flung the plate away and walked off. Mohan says: "God, she was tough, women in those days were tough" (36). But Jaya has a different point of view. She writes: "I saw a despair so great that it would not voice itself. I saw a struggle so bitter that silence was the only weapon. Silence and surrender" (36). Jaya also comes to know about the tragic death of Mohan's mother through Vimla. Vimla's death is also tragic as she had developed ovarian tumour and bleeds herself to death in silence. She does not tell about her problem even to her mother-in-law, as she knew it would be in vain.

Kusum, Jaya's mad cousin, is a deserted wife. Jaya keeps her at home despite the objections from her mother and brothers. After she has recovered a little, her brother takes her away home. But she commits suicide a day before her husband is supposed to take her home. Jaya's help-maid, Jeeja, has her own story of oppression. Her husband also is a drunkard who frequently beats her. She does not protest when her husband takes up another woman because she thinks that she has failed him by not bearing a child to him and so he had every right to remarry. She willingly brings up their son after her husband and his mistress are dead.

He is no different from his father. When the son grows up he too becomes a drunkard who begins to beat his wife. But Jeeja always admonishes his wife whenever she happens to abuse him: "Stop that, don't forget, he keeps the *Kumkum* on your forehead. What is a woman without that?" (53). Then there is Jaya's grandmother *Ajji* who, after she is widowed, keeps herself confined to a room. Jaya's Vanita *mami* too is yet another case. She is barren, and desperately wants a child. She fasts and performs *pujas* and every possible ritual to be blessed with a child, but all is in vain.

Thus, Shashi Deshpande has woven the tragic tales of Jaya's relations and her acquaintances into the texture of the novel, and so the novel inevitably takes on a feminist character. The novel is about gross gender discrimination and inequality prevalent in society, and yet the novelist is opposed to being branded a feminist writer. She may not conform to the conventional concept of feminism, but she does have her own feminist ideas. She says:

> The women in my books are people who come to realize what it is to be a woman in the process of their own lives and the situations they face not through books and theories. I think feminism is an entirely personalized perception. It is when you start questioning preconceived notion about your roles.[7]

In her novels she does not present men as wholly bad and women as wholly good. She is realistic in the sense that her stories are very close to life. She is not writing about Jaya only but also about Mohan, as Jaya says: "I am writing of us" (1). In the novel, Shashi Deshpande does not put the blame of their marital crisis squarely on Mohan's shoulders but also on Jaya's. The novelist suggests that the women should accept their own responsibility for their victimization, instead of putting the blame on others. Jaya mostly blames herself for her suffering. Thus, *That Long Silence* is a serious effort towards "maintaining a credible balance between the sexes."[8]

It is often debated whether or not *That Long Silence* is a feminist novel. Shashi Deshpande is against the labeling of her novels as feminist. She says:

Any woman who writes fiction shows the world as it looks to her protagonist; if the protagonist is a woman, she shows the world as it looks to a woman—to apply the tag of feminist is one way, I have realized, of dismissing the serious concerns of the novel by labeling them, by calling the work propagandist.[9]

The protagonist has raised her voice against the straitjacketed role models of wife and mother, and rebels against the suppression of the age-old patriarchal setup. Thus the novel is a feminist critique as Toril Moi says, "It seeks to expose, not perpetuate patriarchal practises."[10] Although she may not be a formal feminist but she certainly is a potential feminist writer.

NOTES AND REFERENCES

1. Shashi Deshpande, *That Long Silence*, New Delhi: Penguin, 1989.

2. Jasbir Jain (ed.), *Creative Theory: Writers on Writing*, Delhi: Pencraft International, 2000, 210.

3. Adele King, "Effective Portrait," *Debonair*, June 1988, 97.

4. Adele King, "Shashi Deshpande: Portraits of an Indian Woman," *The New Indian Novel in English: A Study of the 1980s*, edited by Viney Kirpal, New Delhi: Allied, 1990, 166.

5. Alladi Uma, "Introduction: A Historical Background," *Woman and her Family, Indian and Afro-American: A Literary Perspective*, New Delhi: Sterling, 1989, 4.

6. Indira Bhatt, "That Long Silence: A Study," *Indian Women Novelists*, edited by R.K. Dhawan, Delhi: Prestige Books, 1991, 157.

7. Shashi Deshpande, Interviewed by Malini Nair, "The Message is Incidental," *Times of India*, No. 25, November 1989.

8. Shashi Deshpande, "The Dilemma of a Woman Writer," *The Literary Criterion*, Vol. 20, No. 4, 1985.

9. *Loc. cit.*

10. Toril Moi, *Sexual/Textual Politics: Feminist Literary Theory*, London: Methuen, 1985, 14.

5

THE BINDING VINE

◆

The Binding Vine[1] is about Urmi, an educated middle-class wife who is grieving over the death of her one-year-old daughter Anu and in the process becomes very sensitive towards the sufferings and sorrows of other people as well. Had she not undergone such a personal loss, perhaps she wouldn't have had any concern with the others. Thus her narrative comprises three tales—one about herself and the other two about Shakuntala, a rape-victim's mother, and Urmi's mother-in-law, Mira, a victim of marital rape.

The novel opens with Urmi grieving over her dead infant daughter, who finds it difficult to let go her memories. For Urmi the loss is terrible and despite the efforts of her friends and family members she clings on to her grief. Although she tries to fight the loss, she feels that forgetting this loss would tantamount to betrayal: "I must reject these memories, I have to conquer them. This is one battle. I have to win if I am to go on living. And yet my victory will carry with it the taint of betrayal. To forget is to betray" (21). It is her intense attachment to her daughter that becomes the cause of her suffering. Her father's death does not shock her much, as she says that her father's is only "a gentle memory" (27). She rejects the idea of having a framed photograph of Anu on the wall: "I don't need a picture to remember her, I can remember every bit of her, every moment of her life" (68). When her friend Lalita asks how many children she has, she says, "Only one. A son." But also gets filled with a sense of guilt as if she was betraying Anu: "How could I, oh God, how could I? That was betrayal, treachery, how could I deny my Anu? [...] only one son [...] how could I?" (106). S. Indira aptly observes: "She clings to her pain and allows her memories of Anu, every small incident to flood her with longing and a great sense of loss."[2]

In such an aggrieved state she happens to meet Shakuntala, mother of a rape-victim, Kalpana. She meets her in the hospital where her sister-in-law, Vanaa works. Kalpana is lying unconscious and her mother thinks that she has met with a car accident. Dr Bhaskar, the doctor in charge, on examination reports that Kalpana has been brutally raped. Her mother Shankuntala's reaction is that of a typical Indian mother bred in an oppressive male-dominated society. She tells Vanaa: "It's not true, you people are trying to blackmail my daughter's name." (58) Gathering from Vanaa and Dr Bhaskar's conversation, she cries in agony and fear. "No, no, no. Tell him, Tai, it's not true, don't tell anyone. I'll never be able to hold up my head again, who'll marry the girl, we're decent people, doctor," she turns to him, "don't tell the police" (58). Most Indian mothers would react in a similar way as they are concerned about their daughters' marriage. The novelist has evocatively laid bare Shakuntala's agony, anger, helplessness and fear. The character has been presented so realistically that it leaves a sense of *deja vu* in the readers. Shakutai (Shakuntala) is in a traumatic state and is sobbing. Urmi escorts her home and from there starts her association with her. She pays regular visits to Shakutai's place to inquire after Kalpana's state. It is during these regular visits that Urmi comes to know about Kalpana from Shakutai. She swings between two extremes; sometimes she is all praise for Kalpana and sometimes puts all the blame on her. Kalpana's character is full of paradoxes. She says:

> She is very smart, that's how she got the job in the shop. Kalpana even learnt how to speak English. People in our chawl used to laugh at her but she didn't care. When she wants something she goes after it, nothing can stop her. She's stubborn, you can't imagine how stubborn she is (92).

She also tells later that Kalpana is secretive in nature as she did not tell her mother even about her pay. Shakutai also expresses her surprise at having given birth to a pretty child like Kalpana. She is full of praise when she talks about her daughter's physical appearance. She says:

She's very pretty, my Kalpana. She's not like me at all.
When she was born, she was so delicate and fair, just
like a doll. I wondered how a woman like me could
have a daughter like that (93).

Though she loves her daughter very much but she puts
all the blame squarely on her shoulders, as she bursts out:
"Cover yourself decently, I kept telling her, men are like
animals. But she went her way. You should have seen her
walking out, head in the air caring for nobody. It's all her
fault, Urmila, all her fault" (14). Although Shakutai puts all
the blame on Kalpana, Urmi finds it difficult to reason out
with her that Kalpana is not responsible in any way for the
brutal rape: "It's not her fault, no, not her fault at all" (147).
She fails to convince Shakutai and is enraged at the fact that
this would lead to the rapist's getting away scot-free. Here we
find her reactions born of the values ingrained in her by the
age-old patriarchal social setup. She was not born with these
values, rather they were embedded into her by the patriarchal
norms. Strictures have been laid for a girl's speech and conduct
so that she doesn't invite men's attention. A girl has to strictly
observe the social norms of how she is to speak, dress and
carry herself in society. She should speak less and if possible
the least as her words might send wrong signals to men.
Similarly her dress should be decent, *i.e.* the contours of her
body should remain suppressed or hidden. A girl is always
asked to behave herself in society and she is not allowed to
interact much with men. Any deviation from these norms
invites the wrath of the family members as it invites danger
of her modesty getting outraged.

Shakutai does not want a report to be lodged with the
police, as she knows that if she does a much greater injustice
awaits her and her daughter. A victim of rape is a loser on
two counts. First, she has been raped, secondly the society
looks down upon such a victim as a *kulta* (a characterless
woman) which leaves the victim in a much miserable plight.

Shashi Deshpande further reveals how the police conduct
in such cases. It is the duty of the police to encourage such
victims to lodge complaints with them so they can punish the
culprit. But the police officer registers the case as a mere

accident to the great shock of Dr Bhaskar, the doctor in charge. He bursts out in anger, and tells Urmi:

> "You could see the marks of his fingers on her arms where he had held her down. And there were huge contusions on her thighs—he must have pinned her down with his knees. And her lips bitten and chewed" (8).

The police officer knows very well that it is a rape case, but he has his own logic. He tells Dr Bhaskar that "She's going to die anyway, so what difference does it make whether on paper, she dies the victim of an accident or a rape" (88). He further adds "her name would be smeared" (88). This is what concerns Shakutai. She knows that it will not only ruin her family's name but also undermine the marriage prospects not only of Kalpana but also of Sandhya, her second daughter. In a society governed by Manu's laws which depict a woman as a being full of "carnal passions, love for ornament, impure desires, wrath, dishonesty, malice and bad conduct,"[3] it is Kalpana who is blamed for as heinous a crime as rape.

We come to know about Shakutai's tragic past. She was deserted by her husband for another woman, and she was left all alone to fend for herself and her children. Dr Bhaskar wonder's how women like her who themselves have had no peace and happiness in marriage could think of marrying away their daughters. Urmi tells Dr Bhaskar that marriage provides security to a woman. She makes an apt remark as in a patriarchal social setup, an unmarried woman is socially vulnerable. Y.S. Sunita Reddy observes: "It is indeed, an irony that to avoid brutalisation of one kind, women willingly submit themselves to a brutality of another kind in the institution of marriage."[4]

Urmi wants justice to be done to Kalpana by bringing the culprit to book. She finds herself a lonely crusader in her fight. Despite opposition from Vanaa and Urmi's mother she takes the matter to the press. She gets the case reopened and with this the identity of the rapist is revealed who is no other than Prabhakar, Shakutai's sister's husband. Sulu gets so guilty conscience that she immolates herself leaving behind a grief-stricken Shakutai.

Shakutai too has her own tragic tale. Soon after her marriage her husband leaves her in her father's home and goes to Bombay on the pretext of earning a livelihood. Six months are past but he does not return. Shakutai becomes impatient and joins her husband in Bombay. Soon she realizes that his husband is lazy and worthless. She gives birth to three children and decides to work for the sake of her children. Despite this her husband deserts her and the children for another woman. She tells Urmi, "That's been the greatest misfortune of my life, Urmila, marrying that man" (110). Since her husband has deserted her, she is to blame not only for her husband's desertion of her but also for anything that goes wrong in the family, for example Kalpana's rape. The society is such that her stoic forbearance of her personal tragedy in marriage and the privations she undergoes in the aftermath are thrown to the winds. She bitterly tells Urmi: "What can you expect, they say, of a girl whose mother has left her husband?" (147). Her putting up with such a husband and fending for herself and her children are of no avail in an oppressive patriarchal social setup.

Shakutai's sister, Sulu, has her own tragic life. She is affectionate and helpful in nature. She helps her as much as possible and even takes upon herself the responsibility of bringing Kalpana up, but that was not to be. Sulu's husband Prabhakar had lusted after her, and Sulu under pressure from her husband had proposed to Shakutai Kalpana's marriage to Prabhakar. Kalpana is infuriated at Sulu and ridicules her. Sulu had been so suppressed after her marriage that she makes such a proposal. Shakutai is all praise for Sulu as very affectionate, helpful and good-natured. Shakutai tells Urmi: "After marriage she changed. She was frightened, always frightened. What if he doesn't like me, what if he throws me out? Nobody should live like that, Urmila, so full of fears" (195). Shashi Deshpande suggests here how sometimes a marriage makes a woman extremely meek and submissive.

Yet another saga of misery, submission and sorrow is that of Urmi's late mother-in-law, Mira. The novelist here ventures into a completely untouched subject of marital rape in Indian Writing in English. She has touched upon the subject in her earlier novel *The Dark Holds No Terrors*, wherein the protagonist Sarita undergoes the traumatic experience of the nightly sexual assaults by her frustrated husband as she is a successful doctor and he an underpaid lecturer. In *The Binding Vine*, Mira has aversion to physical intimacy with her husband and still she has to put up with his obsession for her. She gives voice to her inner self in her poems "in the solitude of an unhappy marriage, who died giving birth to her son at twenty-two" (48). It so happens that many years after her marriage, Urmi receives an old trunk full of books and a few other things from Mira's husband's stepmother, referred to as *Akka*. Among these books Urmi finds Mira's diary which is "not a daily account of her routine life but a communion with herself" (51). When *Akka* hands over Mira's jewellery to Urmi, she says, "They are Kishore's mother's," but while giving books and diaries to her, she says, "Take this, it's Mira's" (48).

Urmi goes through the poems in Mira's diary and gets a glimpse of her troubled marriage. She comes to know from *Akka* how Kishore's father had pursued and married Mira, a college student. The poems and entries in the diary are proof enough for Urmi to conceive the forced sexual activity Mira had to undergo in an incompatible marriage. The extent of her molestation in marriage can be gauged from the following lines:

> But tell me, friend
> did Laxmi too twist brocade tassels
> round her fingers and tremble,
> fearing the coming of the dark-clouded, engulfing
> night. (66)

One of the entries in diary reveals her aversion to sexual activity with her husband. She writes:

> And so it begins. "Please," he says, "Please, I love you." And over and over again until he has done. "I love you." Love! How I hate the word. If this is love it is a terrible thing. (67)

Through her photographs and poems, Urmi gets an image of her mother-in-law as a very lively and intelligent girl snuffed off in a forced, incompatible marriage. Mira's inhibitions about her voicing a desire to become a poet are clear in the following lines:

> Huddled in my cocoon, a somnolent silkworm.
> Will I emerge a beauteous being?
> Or will I, suffocating, cease to exist. (65)

Thus, Shashi Deshpande suggests here that forced violation of a woman's body even in marriage can be as traumatic as rape, even though it is not placed in the same bracket. In her short story "Intrusion" this very concern has been voiced again as the wife finds herself in a situation wherein the husband forces her into the sexual act. The protagonist feels her body has been invaded by her insensitive husband. Here the writer suggests that such incidents are common in the Indian social setup where it is incumbent upon a wife to serve the husband in bed like a prostitute. Thus Mira's diary is a glaring revelation of her "intense dislike of the sexual act with her husband, a physical repulsion for the man she married" (63).

Also in her poems we don't find any mention of her other relations. She does not share this loneliness with others. She has walled herself in like the lady in Kamla Das's "The Sunshine Cat." After marriage to this man she was rechristened Nirmala. Though overtly she does not react but puts down her reaction in these lines:

> Nirmala, they call, I stand statue still,
> Do you build without erasing the old?
> A tablet of rice, a pencil of gold
> Can they make me Nirmala? I am Mira. (101)

With the loss of such selfhood and identity women have to undergo yet another kind of brutalisation. Mira's diary reveals how Venu, a poet, who later rises to become a great figure in Indian literature, subtly snubs her for attempting to write poetry. When Mira gives him some of her poems to read, he says, "Why do you need to write poetry? It is enough for a young woman like you to give birth to children. That is your poetry. Leave the other poetry to us men" (127). It is reflective of the handicaps that women writers often face in a male-dominated society.

Thus, Mira symbolizes the miserable and hopeless lot of innumerable Indian women who suffer silently and their voice remains smothered. The message Shashi Deshpande gives is that the invasion of a woman's body even in marriage can sometimes be as traumatic as rape. A parallel can be drawn between this novel and "Intrusion" a short story by Shashi Deshpande. It's a story about a honeymooning couple wherein the husband forces his yet unprepared wife into the sexual act, which was tantamount to rape. The story is sensitive in the sense that the insensitive husband takes no cognizance of his wife's sense of humiliation.

In case of Harish and Vanaa also we see Vanaa's submission just to keep her marriage intact. She longs for a son and the same is denied to her by her husband. After the birth of a second baby-girl she expresses her desire to Harish for a son. Harish snubs her by saying that she should be one of those women who crave for sons. He also asks her as to why she thinks for sure that the next child would be a son. Despite all these arguments she is ready to take a chance. Urmi gets terribly irritated at her constant refrain "Harish says." She tells her, "Assert yourself, you don't have to crawl before him, do you?" (80). She is also critical of her going out to work and also doing domestic chores all by herself and thus spoiling him and in the process denying love and care to her children. This leads to her daughter, Mandira, to grow with her own notions of the role of a woman as a mother and wife. She thinks that the duty of a woman is to first look after her home and children. She expresses her displeasure at her mother's leaving her and her sister in the care of an *ayah*. She even tells Urmi: "You know Urmi auntie, when I grow up, I'm never going to leave my children to go to work" (72). Her notions are in no way different from the traditional role of a woman.

Shashi Deshpande attempts at satirizing pseudo-feminists like Priti, who are over-enthusiastic about fighting for equal rights for women, but harbour displaced notions about women's freedom. In a case filed by a husband against his wife for restitution of conjugal rights, the court had ruled that the husband couldn't force the wife into physical relationship against her will. Priti is extremely excited whereas Urmi remains sober. Priti says: "Isn't it radical, absolutely earthshaking in this country I mean? Can you imagine the consequences?" (37). But Urmi thinks that one judgement by a single judge, which can be appealed against will make no difference to the entire womankind. She has a pragmatic approach towards their problems and she knows that all such victims cannot go to court. Thus, by making a dig at pseudo-feminists like Priti, she puts forth her own brand of feminism.

Thus, Shashi Deshpande has presented Urmila as a chaste wife whose sympathy for the less fortunate women is sparked off by her daughter's death. Despite her longings and frustrations, Urmila is not a radical feminist but one who, as Basavaraj Naikar opines: "Having entered a *chakravyuha* from which there is no escape, they want to make the best of their given life by hardening themselves to face the harsh realities of life."[5] Besides Deshpande has taken a bold step forward by exploring the working women's needs of the head, heart and the anatomy.

NOTES AND REFERENCES

1. Shashi Deshpande, *The Binding Vine*, New Delhi: Penguin, 1992.
2. S. Indira, "A Bond or Burden? A Study of Shashi Deshpande's *The Binding Vine*," *Indian Women Novelists*, ed. R.K. Dhawan, New Delhi: Prestige Books, 1995, Set III, Vol. 6, 22.
3. Quoted by Neena Arora, *Nayantara Sahgal and Doris Lessing: A Feminist Study in Comparison*, New Delhi: Prestige Books, 1991, 11.
4. Y.S. Sunita Reddy, *A Feminist Perspective on the Novels of Shashi Deshpande*, New Delhi: Prestige Books, 2001, 95.
5. Basavaraj Naikar, "Joys and Sorrows of Womanhood in *The Binding Vine*," *Women in the Novels of Shashi Deshpande*, ed. Suman Bala, New Delhi: Khosla Publishing House, 2001, 126.

6

A Matter of Time

---◆---

Shashi Deshpande has been successful in carving sufficient niche for herself as a feminist writer by articulating the anguish, agony and conflict of the modern, educated Indian women who caught between tradition and modernity struggle for self-expression and individuality.

A Matter of Time[1] deals with the human predicament of three women representing three generations of the same family. For the first time Deshpande makes a man the protagonist of the novel, but this hasn't led her to focusing entirely on the man. As usual she has given expression to their pain, suffering and endurance in marriage.

The novel veers round an urban, middle-class family of Gopal and Sumi with their three daughters—Aru, Charu and Seema. It begins with Gopal entering the house and telling Sumi that he is leaving the house for good. Sumi is unable to react verbally. The next morning she tells about it to her daughter, repeating Gopal's words in toto. She is so shocked with Gopal's action that she lapses into complete silence, trying simultaneously to keep things normal for her daughters. But they feel restless as "Sumi, despite her facade of normality, has a quality about her—a kind of blankness—that makes them uneasy" (10-11). The crisis not only leads to an intense introspection by the women protagonists in the first person narrative but also by the male protagonist Gopal. Although the debate on her identity as a feminist writer still rages, she shows she has the knack to sympathetically delve deep into male protagonists' psyche.

After Gopal's desertion, Shripati, Sumi's father brings them to "Big House"—their parental home. For Sumi's mother,

Kalyani, it's not only a great tragedy, but also a matter of shame and disgrace. She gives a poignant cry: "'No, no, my God, not again.' She begins to cry, sounding so much like an animal" (12). For Sumi, her grief, anger and humiliation are so deep that although she remains calm and composed outwardly but deep within she is very restless. She becomes an enigma for her parents, sister and cousins: "She accepts Gopal's dumb sympathy, Devaki's fierce loyalty, and Ramesh's stupefied bewilderment, as if they are all the same to her" (20). They fail to deal with her apparent stoicism. Sumi's daughters seem to have taken up the threads of their life in the Big House, but she remains totally lost and confused even in her childhood home. She confesses that Gopal's walking out has left such a void that she cannot find her bearings and there are no markers to show her which way she should go. The incident had made a telling effect on her body and soul: "With Gopal's going, it was as if the swift-flowing stream of her being had grown thick and viscous—her movement, her thoughts, her very pulse and heartbeats seemed to have slowed down" (28). Her daughters feel hurt by her apparent stoicism, as they want to share their mother's loss and sorrow. Devaki or Devi even cries to her and tells her, "may be I'm crying because you don't" (107). At this Sumi expresses her sense of great humiliation and loss: "What do I say, Devi? That my husband has left me and I don't know why and may be he doesn't really know, either. And that I'm angry and humiliated and confused" (107).

Gopal's walking out on the family comes as a shock to the readers as well, *i.e.*, why did he marry Sumi in the first place. Theirs is not an arranged one but a love marriage. Gopal asks himself: "Why did I marry Sumi? Because I met her—it's as simple as that" (65-66). Thus, the marriage is devoid of any initial romance, but is the inevitable outcome of a matter-of-fact relationship. The contract was easy and its breach even easier. But their marriage cannot be said to be incompatible as their first physical consummation is fulfilling and gratifying to both. Gopal recounts the union later: "And I knew then that it was for this, this losing yourself in another human being that men give up their dreams of freedom" (223). Deshpande does not assign any tenable reason for Gopal's desertion and the readers remains in the dark as to his motive behind his apparently seeming mindless act.

In the absence of any obvious reasons, Kalyani, Sumi's mother, decides to plead with Gopal to return home. Gopal assures her that Sumi is not at all responsible for his decision, but does not offer any other reason for the act. But Sumi feels hurt when her daughters blame her for Gopal's act of desertion: "Do my daughters blame me for what Gopal has done? Do they think it is my fault? Why can't I open my heart to them?" (23). Sumi, in fact, is trying to come to terms with the hard, painful reality, and expects her daughters also to do the same. Her daughters are also anxious if their father is dead or alive, but Sumi is sure about his being alive and pursuing his own goal. Sumi's sister, Premi, tries to elicit a tenable reason from Gopal, which proves futile. Later Premi comes to know from Aru and Charu that his students at the college had humiliated their father, which could have been the plausible reason for his resignation from his job. But it seems to be so facile an answer that the same is unacceptable to the readers. Deshpande gives no concrete reasons for the act, which suggests that, perhaps, Gopal himself is not sure about the reasons behind his decisive act.

One plausible reason for Gopal's decision is his sense of alienation and loneliness born of his abnormal childhood. Gopal is unable to come to terms with the fact that he was born of the union of his father and his father's brother's wife. A conflict rages in his adolescent mind for the reasons that led to this marriage. Later in life, he happens to read *Hamlet* and draws a parallel between his own and Hamlet's predicament:

> It was when I read *Hamlet*, fortunately much later, that the most terrible version of my parent's story entered my mind [...]. In this story my father became a man succumbing to his passion for his brother's wife, the woman compliant, a pregnancy and a child to come and then after the husband's convenient death (no, I couldn't I just couldn't make my father poison his brother) a marriage of convenience (43).

While his father was alive, he was unable to relate himself to his father as he considered him as his mother's guilty partner. Later, their death leaves a sense of great void in his life. He gets completely shattered at the realization that his sister Sudha and he did not share the same father. And he later reflects, "that was a betrayal that cut away at the foundations of my life" (52). Thus, we see that Gopal has been nurturing a sense of alienation and loneliness since his childhood. He reflects:

All human ties are only a masquerade. Some day, some time, the pretence fails us and we have to face the truth (52).

It is perhaps this realization that has led to his walking out on his family. But Deshpande does not suggest any reason for his renunciation.

Although Gopal's desertion is cause for great worry to Sumi's mother, sister and cousin, but this sudden crisis in her life brings out her great inner strength and self-respecting, strong character. She stoically accepts the humiliation and disgrace of a deserted wife. She raises no fuss over it and lapses into a stone-like silence. Her self-respecting nature makes her refuse all monetary help from close relatives. She takes up a temporary teaching job to fend for herself and her daughters. She is even against staying at the spacious "Big House", her parental home. Though later she moves into the Big House for her daughters' sake. She doesn't rave and rant, sheds no tears and doesn't hanker after sympathy from the relations. Sumi proves that she is made of different stuff as she harbours no grudge against Gopal by setting him completely free to pursue his own purposes by asking Aru not to sue her father for maintenance. She even decides against putting pressure on Gopal to return home for her or for her daughters. Deshpande does not blame either Sumi or Gopal for the abrupt disintegration of this family. She gives a realistic and detached, matter-of-fact depiction of the inner landscape of her men and women characters. Nowhere does she depict him as a careless or carefree husband and father. He has been described as a loving husband and caring father. He is not presented as one shrinking from responsibilities but he has not been idolized either. Subhash K. Jha aptly writes:

"Gopal is not our average cardboard cad but a distressed guilt-ridden husband and father baffled by his own sudden withdrawal from active domesticity."[2] Whosoever may be responsible but Sumi is made to suffer for no fault of hers. Shankar's mother says: "Go back to your husband, he's a good man. If you've done wrong, he'll forgive you. And if he has—women shouldn't have pride" (161). In a tradition-bound social setup like ours elderly women disapprove of such actions objectively without going into the subjectivity of such an incident.

Kalyani-Shripati marriage is at the centre of this novel. Kalyani's plight in marriage is in no way less poignant than that of Sumi's. Deshpande depicts her as an intelligent girl with a promising future, if only she had been allowed to pursue her studies. But the circumstances led her to be married to Shripati. Kalyani's mother, Manorama, had failed to beget a male heir to their property and feared that her husband would marry a second time. She is opposed to Kalyani marrying into a new family, as the property would then go to them. It is under such impervious circumstances that she gets Kalyani married to her brother Shripati just to keep the property within the family. Three children are born of this marriage— Sumi, Premi, and Madhav, a mentally retarded child.

Kalyani's real tragedy begins when her four-year-old son, Madhav, is lost at the railway station while she is to board the train to Bangalore. A son even though retarded, holds so great an importance in the Indian social setup that Shripati doesn't talk to Kalyani for the next thirty years. Soon after the incident, Shripati sends her back to her parents' home with their two daughters. Shripati returns home only after Manorama, her mother-in-law, urges him on her deathbed to return. Although he obliges but not a word is exchanged between them. His return makes no difference to her life or her existence as they live under the same roof as two separate individuals. Sumi reflects: "But for many others this may well be a sound arrangement where husband and wife are living together under the same roof even if there is only silence between them" (167). Here Deshpande lays bare the social compulsion and the vulnerability of such women in a male-dominated society. Even if nothing is left of married life between the husband

and the wife, women suffer in silence just to keep their marriage going. As Sumi reflects of her mother, Kalyani: "But her *kumkum* is intact and she can move in the company of women with the pride of a wife" (167).

Deshpande also reveals the gross injustice meted out to women in matters of property ownership. Sumi is shocked to know that her maternal grandfather's property, which should have been inherited by Kalyani, is bequeathed to her father: "Why did they not give it to her? She finds herself looking into the conundrum of justice, a well so deep, dark and unfathomable, that she draws back" (196). Kalyani had every right to the ownership of the property, but the same is denied to her. Further, Aru is surprised to know that women find no mention in the family tree, although they went through thick and thin while discharging their respective duties to the family. Aru is again surprised when her lawyer-friend, Surekha, whom she meets to sue her father for maintenance, tells her: "Do you know that Manu doesn't mention any duty to maintain a daughter? The duty is towards a wife, parents and sons" (204).

How deeprooted is the desire for a son, is to be witnessed in Kalyani-Manorama relationship. For Manorama, Kalyani is a great disappointment as she gives birth to two baby-girls. She wins favour of her mother when she gives birth to a baby-boy though a mentally retarded one. But that too proves short-lived as she loses her only son in a confusion at a railway station. Deshpande's quote from the Upanishad sums up the Indian psyche:

> Whatever wrong has been done by him,
> His son frees him from it all;
> Therefore he is called a son. By his son
> A father stands firm in this world.
>
> *Brahad-Aranyaka Upanishad* (1.5.17)

In *A Matter of Time* also, she does not leave out the issue of female sexuality. Surpanakha, the mythical Ravana's sister, becomes a symbol of female sexuality. Sumi recalls her mother once say that she was as ugly as Surpanakha. Since then she has been thinking of Surpanakha and the unpleasant incident in which her nose is cut off when she flaunts her love to Rama and Lakshamana. She reflects:

Female sexuality. We're ashamed of owning it, we can't speak of it, not even to our own selves. But Surpanakha was not, she spoke of her desires, she flaunted them. And, therefore, were the men, unused to such women, frightened? Did they feel threatened by her? I think so. Surpanakha, neither ugly nor hideous, but a woman charged with sexuality, not frightened of displaying it (191).

Unlike the earlier novels, Deshpande gives voice to the man's point of view. Gopal's thoughts and feelings are laid bare before us. Motherhood has been given so prominent a place in literature and society that a father's feelings go unnoticed. Gopal's sense of alienation and loneliness since his father's unholy marriage remain so even after his marriage. Earlier also he felt himself like an outsider and even after marriage the feeling does not leave him:

I saw it when Sumi put the baby to her breast. [...] when I looked at them, that they belonged together as I never did. [...] they were together in that magic circle. Woman and child. And I was outside. A man is always an outsider (68).

The mother-son bond is so deep-rooted in a man's psyche that it is nearly impossible to extricate oneself from it. When Shankar expresses his inability to protect his wife from his mother's sharp tongue saying, "She gave me birth, she brought me up, she looked after me", (216) Gopal reflects: "That's a debt we can never repay, it's a burden we can never lay down" (216).

But Shashi Deshpande ends the novel on a tragic note. The reunion of Gopal and Sumi is an unusual one. When he returns she neither cries to him nor abuses him nor does she ask him for any explanations. Everything is normal as Sumi enters the room and finds him having lunch and reading poems.

After lunch also she finds him in a happy mood, laughing and talking to the children. His presence does make difference to the others and her daughters, but for herself she realizes that they can "never be together again" (88). She reflects:

All those days I have been thinking of him as if he has been suspended in space, in nothingness, since he left us. But he has gone on living, his life has moved on, it will go on without me. So has mine. Our lives have diverged, they now move separately (85).

Thus she has come to terms with her present with a new-born understanding to move ahead in life without any bitterness for the man who had been the cause of her humiliation and suffering. Now she is a new woman with a new understanding and consciousness, all set to begin her life anew and confidently as a teacher and creative writer. But this was not to be. Sumi and her father, Shripati, meet their tragic end in a road accident. This gives a philosophical dimension to the novel.

Thus, Deshpande has ventured out of the cordon she had confined herself to and articulates the agony, pain, doubts and fears of her protagonists—male and female alike. She does not fight for justice to women at men's cost, but presents their respective limitations as spouse. In an interview, she tells Vanamala Vishwanath that she desires to reach a stage where "I can write about human beings and not about men or women."[3] And, time and again, she has proved that she remains unsurpassed as a writer of middle-class lives. Shama Futehally aptly observes: "Those who have read and reread Deshpande over the years are united in describing her as a 'middle-class writer.'"[4]

But as Shashi Deshpande's novel is about three women from three generations of the same family and the way they cope with the tragedies in their lives, she is pre-eminently a feminist writer.

NOTES AND REFERENCES

1. Shashi Deshpande, *A Matter of Time,* New Delhi: Penguin, 1996.
2. Subhash K. Jha, "Knotty Problems," *Sunday,* 22-28 December 1996, 54-55.
3. Shashi Deshpande, Interviewed by Vanamala Vishwanath, "A Woman's World [...]. All the Way!," *Literature Alive,* Vol. 1, No. 3, December 1987.
4. Shama Futehally, "Eloquent Silence," *The Hindu,* 19 January 1997, 111.

7
SMALL REMEDIES
◆

Small Remedies[1], Shashi Deshpande's latest novel was published in the year 2000. Here she adopts the structure of a biography within a biography. Madhu Saptarishi, the protagonist, has been commissioned by a publisher to write a biography on a famous classical singer, Savitribai Indorekar, doyenne of the Gwalior Gharana. Like Indu, Sarita, Jaya, Urmi, and Sumi, Madhu also is urban, middle-aged and educated. All these protagonists undergo great suffering in marriage, and when they stand up for themselves they spark off upheaval in the family and society and undergo great embarrassment and humiliation.

Compared to the earlier novels *Small Remedies* has been wrought on a wider canvas. Taking into account the Indian composite culture the structure of the novel encompasses the plurality and diversity of this culture. In this particular novel her characters—male and female—are drawn from different communities and professions. She gives an honest and realistic portrayal of a Maharashtrian Brahmin family. Here, an Anthony Gonsalves, a Hamidabai and Joe are all, in a sense, part of Madhu's extended family.

Shashi Deshpande writes *Small Remedies* at a time when, similar attempts may be witnessed in Salman Rushdie's *The Ground Beneath Her Feet*, Vikram Seth's *An Equal Music* and Bani Babu's *Gandharvi*. Madhu has been commissioned by a publishing house to write a biography of a famous classical singer Savitribai Indorekar, doyenne of the Gwalior Gharana. Writing a novel encompassing such a biography necessitates acquisition of the jargon and idiom of music and a deep understanding and appreciation of the Hindustani classical music. But Deshpande renders the discourse of Hindustani music with great ease in her unfaltering impeccable English.

But Deshpande's main concern is not the Hindustani classical music but the gross gender discrimination prevailing not only in society but the field of classical music as well. Madhu has been asked to write Savitribai's biography wherein she was to be presented as a heroine. But she refuses to present her as such since the latter had been a victim of gender discrimination prevalent in our patriarchal social setup. Imposing the current concept of heroinism on an old woman seemed not only impractical but out of place to Madhu. Instead she presents her as a young woman who had led a sheltered life not only as a child in her parental home but also as a daughter-in-law in an affluent Brahmin family. It is her daring independent nature that makes her seek her own identity and elope with a Muslim *tabla* player to live in a strange town. Although born in a tradition-bound orthodox Brahmin family, she makes a name for herself as a great classical singer. Madhu records how Savitribai felt hurt when her grandmother asked her to stop singing immediately during her performance at a family gathering. Madhu recalls: "In Neemgaon she was 'the singer woman' and there was something derogatory about the words, yes, I can see that now, about the way they said them" (29).

Madhu recalls her as a frail woman and brings her to life by portraying vividly the minute details of her physique. She recalls her as:

> [...] a small sized woman. Even from my child's perspective she had seemed petite. Age and illness have so shrunk her that she's a doll-sized woman now. [...] The skin is fine and delicate, even if it is crinkled like tissue paper. Her arms are slim and firm, but the hands, with their branching of veins, seem incongruously large for those delicate arms (14).

Right from her childhood she had sensed the gross discrimination women had to undergo in a society that had one law for men and another for women. She remembers how men could lead a life of their choice with impunity, while women were jeered at and looked down upon if they showed any deviation from the assigned roles set by society for them. In a society where each family "had its place marked out for it according to religion, caste, money, family background, etc." (138), Savitribai's father with his unconventional ways stood out from society. He was a widower, bringing up a daughter on his own with a male servant at home. He was unconventional in the sense that he would observe no rituals or religious rites and would openly indulge in a drink or two every evening. But all his unorthodox behaviour never invited any censure or disapproval from society. But when it came to Savitribai, it was a different story: "Being a man he could get away with much. He could live the way he wanted to without open censure or disapproval" (139). People are shocked and disapprove of Savitribai's action as she elopes with a *tabla* player to some other town and also begets a child from him.

Even Savitribai's father-in-law is no different. He too could get away with his way of life without any censure or disapproval from society. He had a mistress who was a well-known Thumri singer. He visited her regularly and the people around knew this. It was not much of a secret affair and the woman gossiped about it. It was common knowledge and no furore was ever raised by society there. His choosing a wife from one's own class and mistress from another was quite acceptable, but for a daughter-in-law pursuing a career in classical music was scandalous. Although her father-in-law never discourages her, but Savitribai had to undergo great mental torture as she was treated like an untouchable among women. The little freedom she enjoyed was a great cause for contempt and jealousy to the other women, and they would throw caustic remarks on her way back from her music classes. Only a little deviation from the social norms lays her open to much contempt and ridicule, and also to be treated like an outcast by her own kind. The tortuous experience she undergoes is revealed in the following lines:

> But the subtle cruelty of persistent hostility leaves deeper wounds. There's always the temptation to succumb, to be back to the normal path and be accepted. To resist the temptation speaks of great courage (221).

The gossip surrounding Savitribai in Neemgaon was that a Station Director who had helped her get many contracts with the radio, was her lover. He was a regular visitor to her place. In course of time a daughter is born to her from him. As the child grows up, Madhu recalls how children would tease her by calling the Station Director her *mama*, a euphemism for mother's lover. Though Savitribai, while narrating her life story to Madhu, conceals the fact that she had any lover, but to the small town the Station Director was her lover as he had done many favours to her in the capacity of being a Station Director, and had been visiting her quite frequently. In a patriarchal setup, as Savitribai was "A woman who had left her husband's home" (222), she was considered an immoral woman. Like her father and father-in-law, she too had led a most unorthodox life but had also paid a price for it as a woman. To society, her way of life was inexorable, while her father's or, for that matter, her father-in-law's, was connived at.

Shashi Deshpande, does not delineate her character as a feminist one though she has led a most unconventional of lives. She is ashamed of her youthful indiscretions as while relating her life-story to Madhu, she conceals her intimate association with Ghulam Saab and also the fact that she had a daughter from him. This shows Savitribai's anxiety over her past's reckless action, which she considers a blemish on her character and respectability. She keeps herself aloof from her illegal daughter Munni, lest it should tarnish her image. But this dissociation of hers from her daughter is too much for Madhu as she herself is a devoted and loving mother, grieving over her son's death.

Madhu cannot stomach the fact that Savitribai has kept herself dissociated with her daughter born out of wed-lock and has kept it a most guarded secret. She also gave Munni her name "Indorekar" which she had adopted as her very own identity as singer and which comprises neither her maiden name nor her married one; all this smacks of her possessiveness as she claims her as exclusively her own child, neither her husband's nor her lover's. In her quest for identity she has become overly selfish and possessive, for she gives the child her own identity for her own sake, but disowns her when it comes to sacrificing her hard-earned name for her only child. She loves the child till her own emotional needs get fulfilled but when it comes to Munni's own identity and happiness, she selfishly keeps her out of her life, recoiling under the guise of respectability and a good name. Madhu wonders as to why a woman who had the daring to walk out on her marriage and family, feared to make public the fact that she had borne a child out of wed-lock. All this smacks of her utter selfishness. But we cannot put the blame for all this squarely on her shoulders alone. In a patriarchal society such things are easily said than done. It takes extraordinary courage to make public such facts, and this couldn't have helped Munni in any way. In the West such things have gradually gained acceptance, though not respectability; but in the Indian society, and that too in the older generation, such acceptability was well nigh impossible. And Madhu feels that she could make Savitribai immortal if she made public her most closely guarded secret. Hers would be a story of exemplary courage and sacrifice—a woman sacrificing for one of her own kind, a mother sacrificing her interests for her daughter's. Hers would be a rare example, and this would immortalize her. But this was not to be.

Savitribai eliminates the existence of her daughter from her life to keep her good name and identity intact. She is guilt-ridden and is now ashamed of her past indiscretions and wants to wipe off the memory of such acts from her mind. Meenakshi Indorekar, her daughter, is no exception. She leads the life of a disowned child and is unhappy and ashamed of her existence, as she is a child born of her mother's association with another man. Like her mother, she too wishes her past were dead. She dissociates herself from Ghulam Saab, rejecting him as her father and later does the same to her mother. Madhu recalls how as a child Munni had concocted stories of a lawyer-father living in Pune, and also underwent great mental torture when the neighbourhood girls teased her by asking her about the identity of her real father—was it Ghulam Saab, the Station Director or the man "who lives with your [Munni's] mother?" (77).

She was desperate for a new identity that would cut her off from her past. Once Madhu happens to meet her in a bus, but she refuses to have been familiar to her as her childhood friend. Munni tells Madhu that she was mistaken, and she was not Munni but "Shailaja Joshi."

In her desperate quest for a new identity cut off from her past she has not only given up her mother's identity but refuses to acknowledge any familiarity with her past connections or acquaintances. Unlike her mother, she is a conformist seeking the approval of society. As a child, she has already had a very painful experience as to how society makes life difficult for one who tries to be different or unconventional.

Shashi Deshpande's portrayal of yet another woman character, Leela, Madhu's aunt, is equally commendable and remarkable. She is a communist and a very independent woman. She is not only ahead of her generation but the next generation as well. She was very patriotic, had participated in the Quit India Movement, but as a leftist she was against Gandhi's *Ahimsa* and *Satyagraha* as she considered allowing oneself to be beaten up as ridiculous. She had her own convictions born of her fiercely independent nature. With the passage of time, as she gained experience with age, she regretted some of her actions. Finally she quit the party as she felt that the party's stand in a particular political event was improper. Although she believed in the communist ideology that boasts of making no difference between men and women and declares equal rights and opportunities for both alike, she finds that the party is a victim to male chauvinism which ignores merit in favour of gender.

After the death of her first husband, Vasanth, she takes up a job to become economically independent and also to educate her brother-in-law. Living in the crowded *chawl*s among cotton mills she would work for women suffering from TB. This led to coming into contact with Joe, her second husband, who had set up a clinic for TB patients. He was a widower with two children, spoke flawless English and was well-versed in Literature. Besides Medicine, his other loves were Literature and Music. On the other hand, Leela neither spoke nor knew anything on literature and music.

Though Leela belongs to a different caste, Joe falls head over heels in love with her. She did not believe in caste and the two married. Despite the vast difference in their inherent natures, to Madhu, the two had a wonderful relationship. As Leela was not against inter-caste marriages she had accepted Madhu's parent's marriage and had also offered them to stay with them, as they had nowhere to go.

To Leela all human beings were equal. She was dead against making difference on the basis of class. She was also against the superior status her family gave itself. She was creative and wanted to do things on her own, and saw no wisdom behind her family's holding on to the lands they had inherited.

Though she is a diehard communist supporter, she is a victim of the gross gender discrimination practised in the communist party. She was a hardworking party activist, but when the occasion came, men junior to her reached the higher echelons of power while she was marginalised. She learns the bitter reality that hard work and loyalty to ideology were no merits, and gender was merit unto itself. Madhu gives a telling example of such chauvinism as prevails in all political parties without exception. The widow of a deceased-sitting member was given a ticket to contest in the elections. Leela, a victim of gender discrimination, sarcastically remarks: "It seems you've got to become a widow for them to remember that you exist" (224).

Madhu herself is a victim of the double standards—one for men and the other for women—being practised in society. Only towards the end of the novel do the readers come to know about her real tragedy. Being motherless, she had been brought up by her father and a male servant. She had never felt a lack of mother's love as a child, and does not feel deprived of such love. She had seen the mothers around, leading their monotonous lives of performing household duties and scolding their children all the time. Deshpande does not glorify motherhood, rather presents its realistic picture. Whatever image of motherhood she has, it has been gathered from the movies. But to her surprise the women around her do not "conform to the white-clad, sacrificing sobbing mother of the movies" (183). She finds Savitribai neglecting her daughter, Munni; Ketaki's mother unduly partial to her sons; Sunanda, manipulating and scheming; and her own mother-in-law as very demanding in nature. The real mothers, Madhu finds, are quite different from the mothers in movies. Though motherless as a child, she on her part is a very caring mother, conscious of every little need of her son, Aditya.

Shashi Deshpande, through the marriage and later estrangement between Som and Madhu, gives a stark picture of the patriarchal mind-set of men. Madhu's estrangement from Som occurs prior to her son's death. Once, Madhu, waking up after a nightmare, discloses to him a secret that she had slept with a man when she was fifteen. Although the man had later committed suicide. Som is unable to come to terms with her act. The relationship between the two begins to disintegrate. Madhu fails to comprehend Som as she is unaware of the typical male psychology. In our society where a woman is treated like yet another commodity to be possessed and exclusively consumed for the owner's gratification, a woman becomes the husband's private property. A woman is not to indulge in such acts with others before or after marriage, and is required to serve her husband with single-minded devotion and loyalty. Even if the husband is lecherous, she is not to question him. The society has a sex-centred morality. As Y.S. Sunita Reddy writes: "Our society has been so conditioned as to categorize women as immoral on the slightest deviation on their part from the normal course of behaviour."[2] Thus, Madhu is a victim not only of the double standards of society but of her own innocence. She had slept with Chandru one night in a hotel room in her innocence, and again, in her innocence, she discloses this to Som. Had she spared him the knowledge of her indiscrete act, the relation between the two would have remained normal. But Som with his typical male psychology holds on to this lone act of sex forgetting the fact that he himself has had a full-fledged relation with a married woman before marriage. She reflects: "Purity, chastity and intact hymen—these are the things Som is thinking of, these are the truths that matter" (262). Here, Shashi Deshpande suggests that in our society pre-marital sex could lead to disintegration of marriage.

Although Shashi Deshpande is against being dubbed a feminist writer or a champion of the women's cause, she has brought home her ideas—obviously tilted towards women—

to the readers with great subtlety and skill. We can conclude
with Malati Mathur:

> In portraying struggles of these women for identity, Shashi
> Deshpande waves no feminist banners, launches into
> no rabid diatribes. She drives her point home with great
> subtlety and delicacy.[3]

NOTES AND REFERENCES

1. Shashi Deshpande, *Small Remedies*, New Delhi: Penguin, 2000.
2. Y.S. Sunita Reddy, *A Feminist Perspective on the Novels of Shashi
    Deshpande*, New Delhi: Prestige Books, 2001, 132.
3. Malati Mathur, "Rebels in the Household," *India Today*, 3 April 2000.

8

SHASHI DESHPANDE'S ART

◆

Lord Macaulay wanted the westernization of Indians through the introduction of the English language. Then, he had no inkling that the Indians would ever try their hand at creative writing in English, especially the novel writing. The various commonwealth countries easily adapted this genre with its comparative flexibility and amorphousness. It became a vehicle for the expression of their indigenous ethos. With this started a unique literary phenomenon: a novel having the graces of English language and technique with the indigenous content.

The most challenging task before the Indian English novelist has been the writing of their works in the English language as there is the danger of language getting distorted in giving voice to the Indian ethos. The problem stems from the great difference between the Indian and the Western cultures.

Like the earlier Indian English writers—men and women both—who used the English language depending upon their talent and calibre, Shashi Deshpande also writes in this medium to give voice to women's issues. She writes:

> To those of us who write in English, it is neither a foreign language, nor the language of the colonizer, but the language of creativity. Whether the writing is rootless, alienated or elitist should be judged from the writing, not from the language. My writing comes out of myself, the society I live in. It is shaped, as I am, by my family, my ancestry, the place I was born in, the place I live in, the culture I am steeped in, the fact that the writing is in English changes none of these things.[1]

Shashi Deshpande comes from a middle class, Marathi-Cannadiga background, and was educated in English at a local school in Dharwar, Karnataka and Maharashtra. It is these influences that have played an important role in shaping her writing and use of the English language.

The kind of English language she uses is simple. She does not indulge in showy, bombastic or rhetorical English. It's so simple and straight that it never hinders the reader in any way. Deshpande's concern has been the expression of the Indian middle-class ethos. And her simple, unassuming English reflects it. The English language she uses is of the kind used by an average, middle-class, convent-educated individual. She writes about the middle-class people and the language used is also middle-class English, sometimes a little incorrect by the British standards.

Deshpande's writing is spontaneous. On Vanamala Vishwanath's observation that her writing is not obviously Indian, Deshpande says:

> No, I don't believe in making it obviously Indian. But all this is basically because I'm isolated—I'm not part of any movement and not conscious of readers to impress. To get wider recognition here and abroad, you have to be in the university and places like that with the right contact. I'm an ordinary woman who writes sitting at home. None of these things are within my reach. This has, I believe, done me good, it has given me great freedom. I'm happy with this anonymity. Once you get publicity-conscious, your writing becomes affected. I'm truly happy with this freedom.[2]

Deshpande feels that writing in English is a drawback in this country as it alienates the writer from the mainstream. But she considers English as one of the Indian languages. She says:

> I believe that English writing in this country is a part of our literatures; I consider English as one more of our *bhashas* as Ganesh Devy calls them. I know that our writing comes out of an involvement with this society, out of our experiences here, our readership is now here, and happily our publishers are here as well. Yet, I am disturbed by the recent trend in English writing which in

its pursuits of role models outside, is alienating itself from its roots.[3]

Being an English writer she may have a limited readers' circle compared with the Hindi writers, but this does not make her a non-Indian. She's also against being labeled as Indian-English. She protests:

I am an Indian writer. My language just happens to be English, which cannot be called a foreign language at all because it is so much used in India.[4]

She is also against using the Indian version of English to provide an Indian flavour to her novels:

I do not use Indianisms to make my writing like Indian. I never try to make India look exotic. I do not think of a western audience at all. I belong to Indian literature. I would not like ever to be called an Indo-Anglian writer. I feel strongly about that.[5]

Deshpande is different from the other Indian writers in the sense that she was never educated abroad and is firmly rooted in the Indian soil. She says:

My novels do not have any westerners, for example. They are first about Indian people and the complexities of our lives. Our inner lives and our outer lives and the reconciliation between them. My English is as we use it. I don't make it easier for anyone really. If I make any changes, it's because the novel needs it, not because the reader needs it.[6]

She is fully aware of the problems Indian writers in English face and is of the opinion that they should evolve a language of their own; this will remain distinctively Indian, and yet be English. She has always aimed at the Indian readers and not the Western. Her creative use of the language has been greatly lauded in the *Times Literary Supplement*:

Deshpande eschews linguistic pyrotechnics and formal experimentation, but has sufficient command of her tradition to give the lie to the belief that the English language is incapable of expressing any Indian world other than a cosmopolitan one.[7]

Thus, she is ever vigilant to the issues associated with the contemporary society, and has evolved a literary skill that enables her to present them realistically and convincingly.

It is an acknowledged fact that the novel is "the readiest and most acceptable way of embodying experiences and ideas in the context of our time."[8] The originality or talent lies in the manner a writer uses this genre to bring home his ideas to the readers. Styles and techniques have kept changing with the times. In the past much attention was paid to the plot or story overlooking psychological aspects. But, of late, the modern novelists are doing experimentation, which is far removed from the traditional story telling. Such writers have been dubbed anti-novelists who, as Somerset Maugham writes, "consider the telling of a story for its own sake as a debased form of fiction."[9] According to Paul Verghese, the principal features of the anti-novelist are "lack of an obvious plot; diffused episode; minimal development of character; detailed surface analysis of objects; repetitions; experiments with vocabulary, punctuation and syntax, variations of time sequence, alternative endings and beginnings."[10]

Different authors employ different methods of story telling; hence a narrative technique used by an author holds great significance. The most common method used by the novelists is the plain narrative or story telling wherein the writer holds an omnipresent and omniscient position. Writers who wish to lend a ring of authenticity or reality to their story employ the first person narrative. But this method leads to limit the writer from delving deep into the minds and motives of the other characters. To overcome this limitation Shashi Deshpande has used a combination of the first person and the third person narrative coupled with flashback devices to lend authenticity and credibility to the novel. Deshpande's development as a novelist necessitates a chronological study of the narrative techniques employed by her in her novels. *Roots and Shadows*, Deshpande's first novel is essentially about the protagonist Indu's painful self-analysis. Besides, many other themes also form part of this novel. The theme of bohemianism through the Indu-Naren episode has also been incorporated into the main theme of the novel. The sorry lot of the Indian women in general has been exposed to our gaze through Indu's observations. In a way a large number of themes have been incorporated simultaneously in the novel transmuting it into a coherent whole. Madhu Singh is all praise for Deshpande's skill in interweaving myriad themes into a one close-knit narrative. Comparing *Roots and Shadows* with *That Long Silence*, she points out that the former "is the more powerful of the two. In its succinctness lie its strength and the punch."[11]

Deshpande avoids the simple technique of straightforward narration and employs the flashback method instead to draw her readers' attention. The first chapter deals with the present, but the later chapters move anachronically with the final chapter ending in the present. The narrative technique has earned some criticism from some critics who feel that this leads to confusion in the mind of readers. In novels where the writer is to present a gallery of characters along with their relationships and interactions, it becomes necessary for him to present things in their chronological order and not indulge in too much experimentation. Shama Futehally writes:

> This is a device which is useful either when some element of suspense is needed, or for a novel with a non-narrative structure. For this novel chronological clarity is essential, as the reader already has to cope with an abundance of characters and their complex interactions. The first chapter, where we are faced with all of them simultaneously, and without introduction, is rather confusing.[12]

The entire novel is a first person narrative. The narrator is a young woman writer who returns to her childhood home and finds herself in the maelstrom of family intrigues. Since the protagonist is an educated young woman with liberated and progressive ideas, even ordinary incidents acquire a new meaning. The first person narration helps the writer to probe deep into the mind of the protagonist, her hopes, fears, aspirations, frustrations etc. and thereby highlight the gross gender discrimination prevalent in society. There are reviewers like C.W. Watson, who compare Deshpande to the master storyteller Chekhov:

> Other South Indian writers have been compared to Chekhov. But Shashi Deshpande, in this novel at least,

comes closest to that writer, and the tragi-comedy of
The Cherry Orchard is constantly recalled in the description
of the crumbling house and the squabbling of the family.
The writing is beautifully controlled and avoids the
temptation of sentimentality, which the subject might
suggest and again the control is reminiscent of Chekhov.[13]

In *The Dark Holds No Terrors*, Deshpande shifts the
narrative from the first person to the third person narrative in
every alternate chapter. This double narrative helps to lend
great authenticity to the portrayal of Sarita's inner self.
Deshpande has commendably accomplished the task of giving
a realistic portrayal of the mental trauma Sarita undergoes. In
an interview, she tells how she hit upon the idea of using
double narrative:

> The present is in the third person and the past is in the
> first person. I was doing it throughout in the first. But
> that's often a perspective I use in my short stories. I
> wanted to be more objective. So then I tried it in the
> third. But it wouldn't work at all. Yet I really need not
> distance myself from the narrative in the present,
> otherwise it was going to be far too intense. And then I
> read an American novel by Lisa Alther where she uses
> this method. And the minute I came across her novel I
> thought—let me admit it freely—Oh god, this is how I
> am going to do my novel.[14]

Thus, Deshpande succeeds in the portrayal of Sarita's
mental state with remarkable objectivity. Besides, her art lies
in her amalgamating the past with the present seamlessly
through dreams, nightmares, flashback, reminiscences and
the simple third person narration.

That Long Silence is very close to real life experience, and
achieves its credibility from the fact that the protagonist Jaya
is a well-educated person possessing a literary sensitivity
corresponding with her fictional role. One must realize that it
is a great task to create articulate women characters as they
are nurtured in the culture of silence. This Sahitya Akademi
Award winning novel is about Jaya's hopes, fears, aspirations,
frustrations and later triumph. Y.S. Sunita Reddy observes:

The narrative with its slow unknotting of memories and unravelling of the soul reads like an interior monologue quite similar to the stream of consciousness technique employed by the like of Virginia Woolf.[15]

But Prema Nandkumar maintains that the novel is "not a forbidding stream of consciousness probe in the Virginia Woolf tradition. It is very much a conventional tale full of social realism evoked by links of memory. Not misty recollection but clear-eyed story telling."[16] For the protagonist an objective analysis of what went wrong with her marriage and the reasons for failing as a writer, is a kind of catharsis. The technique is described by the narrator Jaya herself: "All this I've written— it's like one of those multicoloured patchwork quilts the *Kakis* made for any new baby in the family. So many bits and pieces—a crazy conglomeration of sizes, shapes and colours put together."[17]

In *The Binding Vine*, Deshpande adopts a different mode of narration. In *Roots and Shadows, The Dark Holds No Terrors* and *That Long Silence*, Deshpande uses a narrative structure that does not progress chronologically. But instead moves back and forth thematically, gradually narrating one incident after another till the whole story is revealed. But in *The Binding Vine* Deshpande interweaves three individual plots of three different stories about three women of different age, status and education. Urmi narrates the entire story in the first person. To offer a realistic and objective representation of Urmi's mother-in-law Mira's marital experiences, Deshpande has made use of the poetry and writings in her diary and notebooks. She has commendably and brilliantly reconstructed Mira's unspoken humiliation and anguish at being subjected to marital rape through the mouthpiece of Urmi.

Small Remedies has been structured as a biography within a biography. Deshpande delves deep into the traumatic lives of Savitribai Indorekar, Leela, Munni and Madhu by moving her narrative back and forth between the present and the past. The novel works at different levels—the personal, the worldly, women's rights, communal violence, and motherhood. Through the mouthpiece of Urmi, Deshpande has given voice to her own dilemma as a writer—if a biography is an exercise in truth telling, and if it is, whose version must it be? Urmi has been commissioned by a publisher to write Savitribai Indorekar's biography and she is unable to decide whether she should mention only what Savitri tells about herself to Urmi or everything that Urmi knew about her, including her most guarded secrets.

Shashi Deshpande's novels are a realistic representation of women's oppression, and hence are highly susceptible to being labeled as feminist. But she has all along denied any such conscious writing. Even the term 'propaganda' is anathema to her. While Mulk Raj Anand loves to be called a propagandist, Deshpande is against her work being labeled as 'propaganda.' In an interview, she tells Sue Dickman: "Somebody once asked me if I have a social purpose in my writing and I very loudly said 'No,' I have no social purpose, I write because it comes to me."[18]

Shashi Deshpande hates to write propaganda literature. She does not intend to moralize or set forth her own brand of feminism; she is genuinely concerned about people. In yet another interview, she says:

> I hate to write propagandist literature. I think good literature and propaganda don't go together. Any literature written with some viewpoint of proving something rarely turns out to be good literature. Literature comes very spontaneously. When I write I am concerned with people.[19]

But she finds that a lot of men are unsympathetic to her writing while a lot of women are sympathetic. According to her, the reason behind this is "women see a mirror image and men see, perhaps, a deformed image of themselves."[20]

Earlier Deshpande was scornful of the so-called committed writing in literature. But, with the passage of time, she grew mature and realized that all good writing is socially committed writing. She admits:

> There was a time when I was scornful of what is called committed writing. I considered such writing flawed because its being message-oriented diminishes its artistic worth. But now I know that all good writing is socially committed writing, it comes out of a concern for the human predicament. I believe, as Camus says, that the greatness of an artist is measured by the balance the

writer maintains between the values of creation and the values of humanity.[21]

Literary men have always used myth as an important literary devise to enhance the literary effect of their works. While English and other European writers drew much of their mythological symbols from the Christian, pagan and classical myths, Indian English writers have relied much on the stories and symbols from the religious scriptures and epics like the *Mahabharata,* the *Ramayana,* the *Ramacharitamanas,* the *Puranas* the *Upanishads,* and also local legends and folk-lore. Sita and Savitri are the often-used symbols from the Indian mythology.

In *The Dark Holds No Terrors,* Shashi Deshpande has used the mythological tale of Dhruva. Just as Dhruva had been forcibly pushed out of his father's lap by his brother, in the same way Saru also gets her brother out of her way. She had subconsciously wanted her brother to be dead, as she feels herself neglected and redundant because of her brother, and she lets her brother die by drowning.

In *That Long Silence,* Deshpande suggests how innocuous seeming bedtime tales told to children made subtle but indelible impression upon their psyche. Jaya, the protagonist, recollects the fable of the foolish crow and the wise sparrow, which she had often heard as a child. But she does not tell this fable to her children for fear that it would distort their personalities into becoming like the priggish sparrow that was not at all concerned with what went around the world but her children and family.

In *That Long Silence,* Deshpande uses the myths of Sita to articulate Jaya's predicament. She follows her Vanita *mami*'s counsel that a husband is like a sheltering tree that should be kept alive even if one has to water it with deceit and lies. She has emulated Sita's example but Mohan blames her for not being dedicated and loyal towards him. He wanted her to go into hiding, as an enquiry against him has been setup.

In *The Binding Vine,* a mythological parlance can be seen in the stories of Urmila, Mira and Shakuntala and the tales of the mythological characters of their names. The mythological Urmila, Lakshamana's wife, is left in a broken and aggrieved state when Lakshamana leaves for the forest with Lord Rama. In this novel Urmila is greatly aggrieved by the loss of her child. Urmila's mother-in-law Mira, like the mythological Mira remains detached to her husband and both desire relations based on love and not sexual pleasure. Her husband, like her mythological counterpart who had been wronged and deserted by king Dushyanta, deserts Shakuntala or Shakutai.

Although mythological allusions have been used by Shashi Deshpande but she does not consider it to be any conscious or deliberate literary device. In an interview to Lakshmi Holmstrom, she tells:

> I think a number of us do that in India all the time; we relate a great deal of our personal lives, our daily lives, to the myths. We find parallels as a matter of course. And we do this with all the myths, any myth that seems appropriate, whether they were originally about men or women. In that sense it is a part of a language, a grammar that one knows and understands, rather than a conscious literary device.[22]

Although rarely, Shashi Deshpande makes use of irony and satire in her novels, and the presence of the literary ingredients in her novels may not be a deliberate use by Deshpande but there are incidents with these elements. The most striking example is in *That Long Silence*, an event in which Jaya's husband Mohan accuses her of avoiding him in his most adverse situation. Jaya herself was undergoing great mental trauma, and such an allegation throws her off balance. She tries to control herself:

> I must not laugh, I must not laugh [...] even in the midst of my rising hysteria, a warning bell sounded long and clear, I had to control myself, I had to cork in this laughter. But it was too late. I could not hold it any longer. Laughter burst out of me, spilled over, and Mohan stared at me in horror as I rocked helplessly (122).

Later she breaks her silence by recording her story, and thus regains her sanity by relieving herself of her pent up frustrations. Another attempt at irony is Deshpande's creation of the character, Priti, in *The Binding Vine*. When Urmila tells that she was going to publish Mira's story, she was extremely thrilled as the story was going to prove a sensational one. She even plans to adapt the story into a film. Even in Kalpana's rape, her concern is mere hypocrisy as she is concerned with the great publicity the tragedy will generate. But Deshpande can do without these literary ingredients, as her style is very straightforward for irony and satire.

Shashi Deshpande was not taken very seriously in the beginning, as her novels are not concerned with sentimentality and romance. She recalls an incident wherein a publisher had rejected her story. Further advising her to send it to a woman's magazine. She wonders: "Why did the editor say that? It was a good story. I knew that. I was pretty confident about it. It was not a sentimental, romantic love story either, the kind that would fit smugly into a woman's magazine."[23] She probably feels that sentimentality and romance mar the serious concerns of a novel.

NOTES AND REFERENCES

1. Shashi Deshpande, "Language No Bar," *The Sunday Times of India*, Ahmedabad, 23 April 1985, 10.

2. ——, Interviewed by Vanamala Vishwanath, "A Women's World [...] All the Way!," *Literature Alive*, Vol. 1, No. 3, December 1987, 11.

3. ——, "Of Concerns, Of Anxieties," *Indian Literature*, Vol. XXXIX, No. 5, Sept.-October 1996, 108.

4. ——, Interviewed by M.D. Riti, "There is No Looking Back for Shashi Deshpande," *Eve's Weekly*, 18-24 June 1988, 28.

5. *Ibid.*, 28.

6. Shashi Deshpande, "Interview: Shashi Deshpande talks to Lakshmi Holmstrom," *Wasafiri*, No. 17, Spring 1993, 26.

7. Mario Couto, "In Divided Times," rev. of *That Long Silence*, *Times Literary Supplement*, 1 April 1983.

8. R.K. Dhawan, "Preface," *Explorations in Modern English Fiction*, New Delhi: Bahri, 1992, 1.

9. Quoted in Paul Verghese, *Literary Criticism—A Work Book*, Madras: Macmillan India, 1981, 80.

10. *Ibid.*, 80.

11. Madhu Singh, "Intimate and Soul Searching Portrayals of Marriage," rev. of *Roots and Shadows*, *Indian Book Chronicle*, Vol. 18, No. 7, 6 July 1993, 22.

12. Shama Futehally, "Outgrown Flaws," rev. of *Roots and Shadows*, *The Book Review*, March-April 1984.

13. C.W. Watson, "Some Recent Writings from India," rev. of *Roots and Shadows*, Wasafiri, No. 21, Spring 1995, 75.

14. Shashi Deshpande, "Shashi Deshpande talks to Lakshmi Holmstrom," 23-24.

15. Y.S. Sunita Reddy, *A Feminist Perspective on the Novels of Shashi Deshpande*, New Delhi: Prestige Books, 2001, 136.

16. *Ibid.*, 136.

17. Shashi Deshpande, *That Long Silence*, New Delhi: Penguin, 1989, 188.

18. ———, Interviewed by Stanley Carvalho, "Everyone has a Right to Choose a Language", *The Sunday Observer*, No. 11, February 1990.

19. *Ibid.*

20. *Ibid.*

21. Shashi Deshpande, "The Dilemma of a Woman Writer," *The Literary Criterion*, Vol. 20, No. 4, 1985, 35.

22. ———, "Interview: Shashi Deshpande Talks to Lakshmi Holmstrom," 24.

23. ———, "The Dilemma of a Woman Writer," 35.

9

ANITA DESAI, SHASHI DESHPANDE AND BHARATI MUKHERJEE

◆

The chapter focuses on Anita Desai, Shashi Deshpande and Bharati Mukherjee, who bear a curious resemblance to one another in certain respects but are yet very different in many aspects. The three novelists belong to urban upper middle-class, English-educated society, and deal with the world of women. They depict their women characters in all their negative and positive traits. For these women novelists, character takes precedence over plot as they depict the inner landscape of their women protagonists. We see in the women protagonists the "power of women. The deviousness of women. The helplessness of women. The courage of women."[1] These novelists shatter the myth that women find fulfilment in marriage and portray an honest picture of "Women who aspire, attempt and strive to be their true selves."[2]

When Anita Desai's first novel *Cry, The Peacock* was published in 1963, Kamala Markandaya and Ruth Prawer Jhabwala were already well acclaimed novelists. But with Desai, a totally new approach to fiction writing in English by Indian women can be seen. Srinivas Iyengar aptly remarks:

> [...] but in Anita Desai's two novels, the inner climate, the climate of sensibility that clear or rumbles like thunder or suddenly blazes forth like lightning is more compelling than the outer weather, the physical geography or the visible action. Her forte, in other words, is the exploration of sensibility.[3]

Although Desai is of mixed German and Indian parentage, her novels are well entrenched in India soil, as her novels revolve round the working of the mind of her women protagonists. Only those novels of Desai are under review, which veer round women protagonists, i.e. *Cry, The Peacock, Voices in the City, Where Shall We Go This Summer?*, and *Fire on the Mountain*. Shashi Deshpande, like Anita Desai, does objective writing; she maintains a distance between herself and her works. Her novels revolve round the women protagonists' struggle to realize themselves in a patriarchal society. Like Anita Desai and Bharati Mukherjee, she is averse to being dubbed a feminist writer just because her novels are preeminently spun around women characters. She admits her empathy with the fair sex, and says:

> As writing is born out of personal experience, the fact that I am a woman is bound to surface. Besides, only a woman would write my books—they are written from the inside, as it were. Just as a woman cannot get deeply under a man's skin, so too a man cannot fully appreciate the feminine experience.[4]

Bharati Mukherjee, born in a Bengali family in India, has lived in the West, first as a school student and later after marrying a Canadian. Beginning with *The Tiger's Daughter* published in 1971, Mukherjee's novels under consideration articulate the protagonists' experience of the pull of Indian traditions, which are in conflict with Western attitudes, since the protagonists are women, their trauma may be said to stem from the Indian tradition and Western modernity. The common thread that runs through the three novels is the painful acclimatization of oneself to the new society while retaining one's individuality. Unlike Desai and Deshpande, Mukherjee deals with the external world and her novels are not set in the psyche of the protagonists.

Since the three novelists are women and have women protagonists occupying centre-stage in their novels, their feministic outlook is bound to surface. As their roles are traditionally associated with women, the thoughts of these women characters are sure to crop up in their struggle for their identity.

Anita Desai's novels are about the inner worlds of her characters; she has commendably delineated the mental trauma that her protagonists undergo. Like Deshpande, she may not be projecting any feminist ideas or taking any anti-male stand but unconsciously, in her honest and realistic depiction of the husband-wife relationship, she is mouthing concerns very close to feminism. She once admitted to an interviewer:

> I am interested in characters who are not average but have retreated, or have been driven into some extremety of despair and turn against or make a stand against the general current. It is easy to flow with the current, it makes no demands, it costs no effort, but those who cannot follow it [...] know what the demands are, what it costs to meet them.[5]

Maya in *Cry, The Peacock* and Nanda Kaul and Raka in *Fire on the Mountain*, prove the truth of this statement. They fail to tread the path or play the societal roles traditionally assigned to the Indian women. These are introspective and sensitive women protagonists, who live in a world of fantasy like Maya, seek an El Dorado like Sita, flee to a Carignano like Nanda Kaul did or commit suicide like Monisha.

In *Cry, The Peacock*, the protagonist Maya undergoes great mental trauma born of her marriage to a much older, business-like, matter-of-fact Gautama. Owing to an over-sheltered past and father-fixation, she is hypersensitive while Gautama is insensitive towards her sensibilities. Finally, she gets rid of him by killing him by pushing him off the roof. *Voices in the City* is about Monisha who, married into a traditional Bengali family in Calcutta, commits suicide due to the patriarchal claustrophobic atmosphere there. *Where Shall We Go This Summer?* is about Sita, a physically unattractive and hypersensitive women, who flees to Manori to avert giving birth to a fifth child. But her stay at Manori gives her an opportunity to assess her situation objectively. There she realizes that she cannot live forever like this in a make-believe world of her own. She reconciles to her fate affirmatively and decides to accept her existence as a composite whole. *Fire on the Mountain* is about the elderly Nanda Kaul, who retreats to Carignano after having fulfilled her duties to her family. Now, "she asked to be left to the pines and cicadas alone. She wanted no one and nothing else."[6] Her great-granddaughter, to recover from an attack of typhoid, joins her. With a violent father and a suffering mother, Raka lives in a make-believe world of her own. Nanda Kaul is very surprised to find that she demands no attention, and is reticent and aloof. This makes Nanda to recall her past as a selfless wife and mother in her discharging of the traditional societal role of an Indian woman. In *Clear Light of Day*, Tara's visit to her parental home in Delhi gives her an opportunity to assess her past. Since the parents are dead, it is left to Bim to run the old house and tend to the needs of their retarded brother, Baba. Tara rids herself of her alienation by forging a close relationship with Bim.

Anita Desai's protagonists suffer acute mental trauma that stems from their alienation and estrangement from their own self and the society. In a patriarchal setup they find that they are failing to fulfil social expectations or play their traditionally ordained roles.

The problems of Desai's protagonists stem from marital discord and maladjustment. Maya, Tara and Sita dreamed of a happy married life but realized that it was disillusionment like a mirage. Desai does not portray an ideal picture of marriage but gives a realistic presentation in a detached manner. Most marriages in her novels lack love or emotional considerations, which are outright business transactions. Desai's novels represent women's real plight through "incompatible couples—acutely sensitive wives, and dismal, callous, inconsiderate, ill-chosen husbands."[7] In a patriarchal setup, daughters usually agree to their father's choice. Gautama is her father's choice, and she gives her nod to his choice. Maya says:

> [...] my father's proposal that I marry this tall, stooped and knowledgeable friend of his, one might have said that our marriage was grounded upon the friendship of the two men, and the mutual respect in which they held each other, rather than upon anything else.[8]

Gautama is insensitive towards her desires and feelings. The differences in their attitudes are irreconcilable. Toto's death distraughts Maya, whereas Gautama remains detached and insensitive. To Gautama, "lives are trivial and expendable,"[9] and a kind of understanding and companionship was well nigh impossible between the two. She gets rid of such a dead relation—she kills Gautama by pushing him off the terrace. She does so in a detached mood as his death would not matter her much for he had "never lived and never would."[10]

Monisha's plight in marriage is much worse than Maya's. Her marriage is doomed right from the very beginning. She is married into a family unlike hers. Aunt Lila realizes that they were "a respectable, middle-class congress family, completely unsuitable to Monisha's tastes and inclination."[11] Anita wonders:

> [...] Monisha had been married to this boring nonentity, this blind moralist, this complacent quoter [...] minute minded and limited official.[12]

Whatever be the reasons for this marriage, Monisha is very unhappy in Jiban's house. She remains confined in his house, segregated from the city of Calcutta. The worse past of her existence is that she even feels estranged and lonely in Jiban's house. Monisha says, "They have indoor minds, starless and darkless."[13] To her life becomes so stifled and meaningless that she finally commits suicide. Thus, Maya and Monisha seek a release from their marital-discord by an extreme step.

Sita in *Where Shall We Go This Summer?* marries her father's choice who is his father's friend Deedar's son. After her father's death, she becomes lonely when her brother and sister leave her. At this juncture, her father's friend Deedar's son comes "to cremate her father, shut the house, fetch her away, send her to college, install her in a college hostel and finally out of pity, out of lust, out of a sudden will for adventure, and because it was inevitable—married her."[14] And, to her, marriage proves to be a great disappointment; gradually she loses her zest for life. She becomes so fed up with him and her own intolerable plight that she runs away to Manori to escape from her "duties and responsibilities, from order and routine, from life and city."[15] At Manori, she realizes "what a farce marriage was, all human relations were."[16] The cause of her real grief is that "she was bored, dull, unhappy, frantic. She could hardly believe that although they lived so close together, he did not even know this basic fact of her existence."[17] Towards the end of her novel she realizes that she cannot stay on at Manori indefinitely, also the fact that the child could not be kept inside her womb forever. At the end of the novel, she decides to go back and face the facts of life however bitter they may be. Thus, Sita evolves into a more mature woman than Maya and Monisha who had failed to come to terms with their lives.

In *Fire on the Mountain* Nanda Kaul has been portrayed as a selfless and dutiful wife who later reminisces her past which is only unpleasant to her. She maintains a cool exterior as a devoted wife, in spite of being aware of her husband's liaison with Miss David. She accepts her lot stoically as she considered their house as "his house, never hers."[18] After her husband's death, she moves alone to Carignano, where she gets plenty of time to reconsider her past. She had played out her role of an ideal wife and mother to perfection. At this late stage at Carignano, she feels that marriage had been surely an unpleasant experience. Her daughter also is a victim of a marriage gone haywire, as her husband is very violent in nature.

In *Clear Light of Day*, Tara marries Bakul as means of escape from her stifling existence in her house and family. She considers the reasons for marrying Bakul only after marriage. She was so impressed by Bakul that she fell in love with him, and could not pause to consider her reasons for marrying him:

> I didn't think of it that way then [...]. At that time I was just swept off my feet [...]. Bakul was so much older and so impressive, wasn't he? And then, he picked me, paid me attention—it seemed too wonderful and I was overwhelmed.[19]

But there is no marital discord with Bakul as she had no expectations from the institution of marriage. Another protagonist is Bim. As a child she thought: "I can think of hundreds of things to do instead. I won't marry."[20] She was determined to lead her own kind of life without succumbing to the social pressure.

Desai's protagonists break away from the traditional role model. They have a different attitude towards child bearing and motherhood. As Kamini Dinesh observes that they can be read as a "negation of the role model."[21] In Desai's novels a mother is never presented as one seeking fulfilment in her role. Nanda Kaul never relished the role of a mother, though she discharged the duties of a wife and mother very well. While living in loneliness at Carignano, she recalls her experiences as wife and mother with great horror. She sees her past as something that is "not bare and shining as the plains below, but like the gorge cluttered, choked and blackened with the heads of children and grand children, servants and guests, all restlessly surging, clamouring about her."[22] Motherhood was never an enjoyable or satisfying experience to her: "It had been a religious calling she had believed in till she found it fake. It had been a vocation that one day went dull and drought-struck as though its spring had dried up."[23]

To Sita also, motherhood is not a pleasing but frustrating experience. Thus, at her fifth pregnancy she is full of "paranoiac show of rage, fear and revolt."[24] She reacts by saying, "It is not easier. It's harder, harder, it's unbearable."[25] To her the circumstances become so intolerable that she tries to run away from her family, home and familiar surroundings, but she is against the idea of an abortion: "I want to keep it [...] what I'm doing is trying to escape from the madness here, escape to a place where it might be possible to be sane again."[26] Her four children misunderstand her. They are no solace to her. To Sita, "children meant only anxiety, concern— pessimism. Not just happiness, what other women call happiness is just—just sentimentality."[27]

Bim and Tara also had been neglected by their mother. Both have only unpleasant memories of their mother, as she was always busy with her bridge sessions at the club. The mothers being unworthy of emulation, none of the protagonists consider motherhood to be an essential fact of their lives.

Ila Das, Nanda Kaul's friend in *Fire on the Mountain* is a pitiable, helpless woman, who holds on to her self-righteousness even in her most unfavourable circumstances. She has reached the tragic, lonely situation due to her irresponsible brothers and her wrong upbringing. In Nanda Kaul's opinion: "There had never been anyone more doomed, more menaced than she and how she survived it all—just by the barest skin of her teeth,"[28] was very surprising.

Desai presents Ila Das as a foil to Nanda Kaul. In spite of her pitiable circumstances, Ila Das shows a concern for others while Nanda Kaul thinks only for herself. Ila continues to believe in her ideals; she thinks she can work for the betterment of the villages by reaching out to their innate goodness. At the end of the novel, Ila is raped and murdered. The patriarchal setup brings her to a more pitiable end: "crushed back, crushed down into the earth, she lay raped, broken, still and finished."[29]

Desai's protagonists belong to the upper class of urban India. Excepting Bim, the other protagonists do not regard economic independence as an important issue. Directly or indirectly they question the accepted codes of a patriarchal society. They question the roles defined for them by the traditional social conventions. They have no faith or lose the same in the institution of marriage or the joint family.

Desai's protagonists find themselves helpless adapting and adjusting themselves to their circumstances, and many of them meet their unnatural end. It is in *Clear Light of Day* that Desai introduces an intelligent independent-minded protagonist, Bim, who risks entering the traditional male domain, choosing a career and earning her livelihood. Bim succeeds in extricating herself from the constricting influences of her family, breaking off the shackles of her past and bringing order to her life.

Bharati Mukherjee's protagonists too undergo great privations due to their beleaguered circumstances. *The Tiger's Daughter* is about Tara, a rich industrialist's daughter, who returns to Calcutta after seven years in the U.S. Although she grew up in Calcutta, she fails to fit into its culture. She finds that she is as much of an alien at home as she was abroad. *Wife* is about the pre- and post-marital experiences of Dimple Dasgupta—an ordinary looking, middle-class girl, who is unable to accept the humdrum and meaningless existence that marriage leads her into. Her moving to New York makes matters worse. She plans suicide in a dozen different ways but ends up murdering her husband. Jasmine is the story of an uneducated Punjab peasant girl Jasmine, who travels from a little known place in Punjab to the U.S. to fulfil her dream of freedom by dint of her courage and determination. The beauty and brutality of America have been rendered commendably through the experience of Jasmine.

Bharati Mukherjee's feminism stems from the fact that the three protagonists differ in their perception of their roles in society and their expectation of life. Tara considers her marriage to David as a gesture of freedom, but comes to realize that such a freedom presupposes a bondage, which she is not willing to accept. She is dutiful daughter to the Bengal tiger, and wants to become a dutiful wife in the traditional mould. She wants to keep him in good humour and is wary of his comments or criticism. Though David often "accused her of stupid inanities and callousness,"[30] but she doesn't react with any "confession, reproof or rebuttal."[31] Despite her seven-year stay abroad, she hasn't matured or sought an identity of her own. She finds it difficult to protect herself from people like Tuntunwala. She returns to David for safety and security. In patriarchal social setup most girls are meek and submissive. Their socialization fails them in their endeavour to seek their individuality or an identity. Rooted firmly in the patriarchal traditional mould, she is unable to adapt herself to the conditions of the land she emigrated to.

Dimple also, like Tara, with no life apart from that of being a wife, fails to acquire an individuality of her own. Her upbringing is such that she's romantic in nature. She expects her husband to be "infallible, intractable, godlike, but with boyish charm."[32] Her romantic expectations lead to terrible disappointments in Dimple's marital life.

Child bearing and child rearing restrict the freedom of women and an abortion is often seen as a way of protesting against gender related roles by feminist characters. To get rid of the baby she "skipped rope until her legs grew numb and her stomach burned."[33] Even later, Dimple has no qualms about the incident. Although she had failed to develop a meaningful relationship with her husband, Dimple continues to perform the traditional role of a dutiful wife like leaving the tastier portion of the meat for her husband. Dimple aspires to the traditional role assigned to her by society, but fails to achieve them because of her innate weaknesses; her final protest is the killing of her husband.

Bharati Mukherjee gives gender-role related titles to her first two novels, *The Tiger's Daughter* and *The Wife*. The third one, *Jasmine*, suggests a sea change in the title itself. Jasmine hails from Hasnapur from Punjab, where "daughters were curses."[34] But she succeeds to rise above being merely a daughter or a wife. At each stage she is faced with a loss of identity, and she is able to evolve an identity. She is the dowry-less fifth daughter of a post-partition, riot-affected farmer in a non-de script village of Punjab. Circumstances lead her to become the ambitious wife of an even more ambitious budding engineer who has plans to emigrate to the U.S. In her village also she faced the discrimination that every girl-child in rural India has to. As she was a curse to her mother "the ruby-red choker of bruise around my [her] throat and sapphire fingerprints on my [her] collarbone"[35] indicate that her mother had tried hard to spare her the life of a dowry-less bride. At school she does well in studies and is a favourite of the schoolmaster. She belongs to a society where "bad luck dogged dowry-less wives, rebellious wives, barren wives. They fell into wells, they got run over by trains, they burned to death boiling milk on kerosene stoves."[36]

She is married to Prakash, a modern, city-bred man, and this opens up a new vista of life for her. But he imposes himself on her, flouts all age-old traditions. But he's against her becoming a mother: "We aren't going to spawn! We aren't ignorant peasants."[37] After Prakash's death, she decides to go to the U.S. alone, with the purpose of committing *suttee* in the campus of the university her husband had planned to enrol in. She plans to travel to the U.S. in spite of many hurdles. Later, when she is raped by Half-Face, she emerges as Mata Kali—an avenger of evil. Her desire to be dutiful wife and later mother finds fulfilment in ways different from what she had expected. Jasmine successfully experiences the traditional roles of a woman as a caretaker to Duff and a foster mother to Du, and a partner to Taylor, a caring wife. The choices that Jasmine makes are final proof of her capability for decision making and desire to live her life according to her own rules, which is evident when she leaves Bud for Taylor as she is "caught between the promise of America and old-world dutifulness."[38] Indira Nityanandam aptly observes:

It is only Jasmine who shows an undaunted spirit and enthusiasm in learning to survive against all odds. The daughter, Tara, and the wife, Dimple, evolve into Jasmine—an individual with a personality unbound by traditional limitations.[39]

Desai, Deshpande and Mukherjee portray the world of the women of today. They create women characters who struggle hard against the social setup to acquire an identity and individuality of their own. All the three novelists deal with middle class urban women, excepting Jasmine who originally belongs to rural Punjab. Deshpande's protagonists show a more realistic and mature approach than the protagonists in Desai's novels in the assessment of their situation or condition in society. Sarita, Jaya and Indu feel hemmed in by the social shackles, which bind them to traditional attitudes and expectations, and yet they try to achieve independence within that framework. To her, marriage means constricting bonds but are not against the social institution like marriage. They are able to come to terms with themselves and the social reality around them by seeking a realizable goal within the accepted codes of society. While Desai's protagonists fail to come to terms with the reality around them. Either they commit suicide like Maya and Monisha, or live a life of glorious isolation like Nanda Kaul, or flee to a dream world like Sita.

Most of the protagonists do not have a separate identity or role outside their home. They are not economically independent as they have no jobs, and this proves a great hurdle to their self-realization. Sarita, who is a successful doctor, finds her personal expectations and familial duties in conflict. Jaya and Indu, too, attempt to find a role outside the family but soon realize that the restricting bonds of the family hinder them in the process. Even their desire to express themselves through writing is suppressed or hindered. The traditional male fails to realize that a woman needs to fulfil her real identity not only within but also outside the domestic sphere. In Desai's novel, it is with Bim that we find the capability to move out of her cloistered self at home into the world outside and lead life of her choice. She avoids marriage and achieves both independence and self-realization. But

Mukherjee's protagonists do not consider economic independence as a necessity or even a possibility.

The three novelists give a pre-eminent position to marriage and marital relationships in their novels. In Deshpande's novels, discords or disappointments in marital relationship impel introspection in the protagonists. They don't disregard the importance of marriage as a social institution, and seek solutions to their marital problems with marriage. They seek a balanced, practical approach to their problems. They have the courage born of their being honest to themselves after an objective appraisal of their situation. They don't blame the others or their husbands for their troubles, but also themselves. Their desire to seek solutions to their problems leads to their temporary withdrawal from their families, followed by an objective appraisal of the whole problem. They are no rebels to flout the social norms. They are traditional in their approach as they strive to seek identity and self-realization upholding social conventions and institution. There are women who are individuals with awareness of their rights and duties; they have legitimate several passions and who expect an independent, autonomous existence. Their circumstances lead to their becoming mentally mature who finally consider marital relationship as worthy of preservation.

Desai's protagonists show a different approach to the institution of marriage. Whether it be Maya or Sita, marriage never provides any sense of security, freedom or happiness to their protagonists. Being disappointed, Desai's protagonists react to the situations they are faced with. They are sensitive and unhappy to the point of being neurotic. Marriage never appears to hold any sanctity for them; hence, for them the preserving of marital relationship does not hold much significance. Desai's women characters lack the inner strength and courage that is characteristic of Deshpande's women. They fail to find a solution to their marital problems, because they have no identity of their own, and seriously lack an honest introspection of their situation. While Deshpande's novels end on a positive note, Desai's end on a nihilistic note, with only Sita growing into a responsible individual with a clear perception of her duties towards marriage and her family. Even Nanda Kaul has been lying to herself all her married life. Those characters do indulge in a little introspection now and then, but the honesty is missing. By comparison Deshpande's protagonists are more representative of the Indian women of the present day.

Bharati Mukherjee's protagonists differ in their attitudes about marriage and marital relationships. All the three protagonists have different expectations from marriage; like Dimple, Tara does not consider marriage to be the ultimate goal. Tara marries David, a non-Indian, but he is a distant presence who does not affect the tenor of the novel or the depiction of the protagonist. Tara does not seriously consider her marriage, as she has no expectations from it or David. She has no conflicting feelings or tensions about her partner or her marriage. She knows that she can never reveal her innermost thoughts to her husband. There is no marital discord as such, but whatever conflict there is between the two is due to their different upbringing. Tara has her roots in the Indian patriarchal tradition, while David is a product of the ultra-modern Western world. To Dimple her marriage is a total disappointment. She has romantic notions about marriage, which are belied soon after her marriage. She finds no romance and thrill in her marriage and she pins all blame on her husband, Amit. To Jasmine, each marriage serves a different purpose and fulfils a unique need. Her marriage with Prakash holds great significance as it brought her out of the traditional, feudal setup of rural Punjab. Her belief that marriage is sacrosanct undergoes a total change in the U.S. She accepts the idea of living with Bud without marrying him, and even carries her child. Yet, she tries to be a dutiful wife to him. When she walks out with Taylor, at the end of the novel, she appears ready to settle down to a happily married life with him. Marriage provides Jasmine a greater fulfilment and happiness.

The three novelists also deal with the theme of extra-marital relationship, which is closely related to marriage. Shashi Deshpande's protagonists have extra-marital attractions, *i.e.*, Sarita for Boozie and Padmakar, Indu for Naren, and Jaya for Kamat. These protagonists see their attractions objectively, and do not allow themselves to be bogged down by any feeling of guilt. Indu does not consider that her relationship with Naren had anything to do with Jayant. Lack of any meaningful communication with their spouses leads to their developing such relationships. But soon they realize the futility and absurdity of such relations. Such attractions are short-lived and have no serious impact on their marriage, on the other hand Desai's protagonists don't have any kind of extra-marital attachments. Despite their claustrophobic marital life, her protagonists never try to seek release in a relationship outside their marriage. Nanda Kaul in *Fire on the Mountain* is deeply hurt by her husband's liaison with one Miss David. But these protagonists prefer to follow the traditional line. While Bharati Mukherjee's protagonists, exposed to Western society and attitudes are different from Desai's protagonists. Tara remains the traditional, monogamous wife while she is far away from David. Even Dimple's flirtation with Milt is mild and only half-hearted. Whereas Jasmine doesn't flirt with Bud or Taylor but has full relationship with the two. She considers her relationships with both as serious, and remains dutiful towards both. Neither is a temporary extra-marital relationship. At the end, she leaves Bud and walks out with Taylor on moral grounds.

These protagonists have no predilection for motherhood. They all evade performing the duties of a mother. Sita and Dimple are disinclined to bearing a child for their own reasons. Sita does not want to abort the child but keep it in her womb forever by working a miracle. She considers the unborn child an "unfinished business" which could "clutter up the preparations for going abroad."[40] Hence, she decides to skip rope to induce an abortion. Monisha does not give much thought to motherhood or her incapacity to bear a child. Some of these protagonists were greatly disappointed by their mother as they had failed to be ideal mothers. Seeing that motherhood had no glamour or thrill about it, these protagonists are not keen on playing the role of a mother.

Shashi Deshpande's protagonists do not show any perceptible progress in terms of development of character. Sarita, Jaya and Indu face similar problems and achieve a similar self-realization. They withdraw from their families for a while; analyze their circumstances objectively without any external aid or advice. Then they return to the home and family knowing full well as to what is to be expected of themselves and their respective spouses.

Desai's protagonists show a clear progress from Maya's dreams to Bim's self-realization and Sita's acceptance of the inevitable roles for a woman. Maya and Monisha are dreamy-eyed and have misplaced expectations from their husbands. Nanda Kaul realizes the truth about herself at a very late stage that she had only been lying to herself as a wife and mother. But Sita learns to accept what she cannot change. She returns to her flat in Bombay with Raman and her children. Usha Bande aptly remarks: "Symbolically, when Sita walks back home placing her feet in Raman's foot-marks on the sand, she decides to contribute positively to their lives."[41] Bim shows a development during the course of the novel. She is able to view her circumstances objectively only after she gets rid of all cobwebs of the past. She makes hard choices not in consonance with the traditionally imposed societal roles, and, unlike other Desai's protagonists succeeds in achieving an identity of her own.

Bharati Mukherjee's protagonists in most respects differ from Desai's and Deshpande's protagonists. Her protagonists are unlike each other socially, economically and temperamentally. Tara is a businessman's daughter sent abroad to study, Dimple is a middle-class, ordinary looking girl while Jasmine is a rural girl with the courage and determination to face the wide world on her own. Tara lives abroad with a husband of her choice, but she fails to protect herself from Mr Tuntunwala. She lacks the capacity to react properly to her situations, which is so necessary for an individual living abroad. At Calcutta she wants to remain a dutiful daughter of her parents, but when the situation there becomes oppressive, she prefers to flee to her husband. Maya and Monisha too lack the strength to face situations when they crop up. It is only Jasmine who shows the strength to face crisis, overcome obstacles, and the capacity to adapt herself to the ever-changing conditions. She shows a strength and adaptability which we find missing in Mukherjee's other protagonists.

The mental states of Maya and Dimple can be gauged by their murder of their husbands Gautama and Amit respectively. Maya kills her husband by pushing him off the roof. Since

Toto's death Maya had been anxious about the albino astrologer's prediction of the fourth year of their marriage. She had become convinced that only one of them would survive the fourth year. In her eyes "Gautama had never lived, and never would."[42] Later Maya falls down from the balcony pulling her mother-in-law along. On the other hand, Dimple's murder of Amit proves that Dimple had lost the capacity to distinguish between life presented on the T.V. and in real life. When she murders Amit by stabbing him in the kitchen, she believes that she would get away with it like the "Women on television got away with murder."[43] She had thought over various methods of suicide like hitting herself on the head with a shovel, freezing to death, cutting her jugular vein etc. She had become very obsessed with death and suicide. Monisha too commits suicide, as she wanted to extricate herself from her claustrophobic existence. Nanda Kaul's death is caused by the great shock she experiences on hearing the news of Ila Das's rape and murder. These women lack the courage and strength to face the harsh realities of life.

These protagonists lack a cordial relationship with their mothers. Sarita articulates her dislike for her mother: "If you are a women, I don't want to be one."[44] Jaya likes her father more than she does her mothers. Even Indu dislikes Akka's domination. Maya and Sita didn't remember their mothers, and Tara and Bim were neglected by their mother. Nanda Kaul couldn't prove to be an ideal mother, and Raka's mother was reduced to a pitiable condition by her violent husband. Tara is the tiger's daughter and has no intimacy with her mother.

All three—Desai, Deshpande and Mukherjee—are against being dubbed as feminist writers. But they do present their own brand of feminism in very subtle ways. These novelists have presented a woman's world from a woman's point of view, which shows their serious concern over women's issues. Deshpande admits: "I am a woman and I do write about women, and I'm going to say it loudly, I don't want to dissociate myself."[45] None of the novels discussed have well-developed male characters, and are seen only in relation to the protagonists as husbands or fathers or brothers. In

Deshpande's novels husbands have been indirectly made responsible for their wives' troubles. In Desai's novels, Gautama's and Raman's rational minds are in sharp contrast to their hyper-sensitive wives. While Monisha and Nanda Kaul undergo utter loneliness because of their lack of communication with their husbands. In Bharati Mukherjee's novels, husbands play a less important role in the protagonists' lives, when compared to Desai's and Deshpande's novels. In Deshpande's novels father-daughter relationship is better placed than the husband-wife relationship. Sarita's father helps her to rid herself of guilt-consciousness; Jaya loves her father, as he would always encourage her by making her feel special. Her father treats Maya like a princess, and she assesses every other male relation in comparison to her father. In Mukherjee's novels, fathers have been portrayed as being fully involved in their duties, whether it is sending Tara to U.S. for her studies or groom hunting for Dimple and Jasmine.

A study of these three contemporary novelists reveals some interesting similarities and differences among their protagonists, male characters and the society they portray. We find that these novelists portray a wide spectrum of contemporary Indian woman who are truly representative of the average urban Indian woman of today. These novelists have commendably given a realistic representation of the consciousness of their protagonists. Each protagonist strives for an identity of her own, aside from the traditionally ordained straitjacketed roles of daughter, wife and mother. Despite the common traits, these protagonists have their own significant difference, from the others.

Though Desai's protagonists dare to say 'no' to their traumatic existence, but fail to find any resolution to their problems, with the exception of Bim. The earlier characters were not normal characters, as Desai admits, and death is the only solution to their problems. In *Cry, The Peacock*, the astrologer's prediction keeps ringing in Maya's ears. Her hypersensitive disposition makes her impatient with Gautama's rational logic and staid nature. Her fear of death and the desire to live leads to such neurotic mental state that she commits homicide and later suicide. In *Voices in the City*, Monisha desires to lead a life of freedom that is denied in

Jiban's joint-family home in Calcutta. She compares her present life with her childhood life led in the open spaces of Kalimpong. This makes her life intolerable and meaningless, and she commits suicide. Maya and Monisha lack the courage and maturity to accept the harsh realities of life. In *Fire on the Mountain*, Nanda Kaul retreats to the solitude of Carignano in an attempt to forget her unpleasant memories of her unhappy marriage. All through her life she has been pretending to be a happily married woman, and only towards the end of the novel does she admit to herself that it wasn't so. Under the guise of a dutiful and dedicated wife, she connives at her husband's life-long affair with another woman. After Ila's rape and murder she is totally broken, and later commits suicide.

In *Where Shall We Go This Summer?*, Sita flees to Manori to escape her wretched lot born of her romantic, unrealistic expectations, and also to avoid giving birth to the child in her womb by some miracle. She lacks the courage and inclination to take on family responsibilities. When the truth dawns upon her, she returns to her family and home. In *Clear Light of Day*, Bim has the courage, strength and intelligence to fulfil her dream of an identity and self-realization. She proves that she can fend for herself and support the family, without letting the impervious circumstances overwhelm her. Bim is representative of the emancipated, independent woman Anita Desai seeks to portray. Being neither a defeatist nor an escapist, Bim is a practical-minded woman who finds solutions within limitations of her life. She heralds the arrival of Deshpande's protagonists.

Shashi Deshpande's protagonists are stronger than Desai's protagonists. They refuse to sacrifice their individuality for the sake of upholding the traditional role models laid down by society for women. But they attempt to resolve their problems by a process of temporary withdrawal. In *The Dark Holds No Terrors*, Sarita returns to her paternal home to escape from her husband Manohar's sadism. This temporary withdrawal helps her view her situation objectively. Besides being merely a daughter, sister, wife or mother, she evolves into an individual with her own legitimate expectations of life. In *Roots and Shadows*, Indu frees herself of the constricting traditional role of a wife and mother, and dons the mantle of the family matriarch at Akka's bidding. She realizes that her husband Jayant need not determine the role she should play in her own and other people's lives. She has now matured into an individual with an identity of her own, and who can choose to live life of her own choice. In *That Long Silence*, Jaya undergoes great mental trauma because she has refused to go into hiding with her husband as an enquiry against his financial irregularities is on. Gandhari-like she kept her eyes shut to his husband's illegal earnings at office. Even her journalistic writings are circumscribed by her husband's likes and dislikes. Finally she is able to evaluate her expectations of life, and comes out with a very revealing novel. After having rejected traditional role models, Deshpande's protagonists display great strength and courage in evolving their own role models as per the requirement of their social milieu. Comparatively, Desai's protagonists remain static, while Deshpande's protagonists display a tangible development during the course of the novel. They go through a process of self-examination before they reach self-actualization. Thus, Shashi Deshpande has been successful in creating strong women protagonists who refuse to get crushed under the weight of their personal tragedies, and face life with great courage and strength. Comparatively, they appear to be more life-like and more akin to the educated, middle-class, urban Indian woman of today.

While Deshpande's protagonists move out of their home, Mukherjee's protagonists move into an even wider world by leaving Indian shores for abroad. They try to build a home away from home but fail to break themselves free of the traditional Indian ideas and attitudes. In *The Tiger's Daughter*, Tara's sense of rootlessness is the main cause of her feeling homesick both at Vassar and at Calcutta. She is too Western to accept life in Calcutta, and too Indian to be happy and contented in the U.S. Despite the lure of the West and an American husband, she fails to develop a sense of belonging to the West. Dimple in *Wife* is a hypersensitive and neurotic character. She's unrealistic in expecting the U.S. to be an El Dorado. Amit is an average individual who cannot attain success in the U.S. overnight. Her condition is further aggravated by the sense of loneliness that she faces in the U.S. and her mental state becomes so deranged that she commits cold-blooded murder of Amit. Jasmine in *Jasmine* is very practical and ambitious by disposition who keeps adapting herself to her changing circumstances. She never lets her past become an impediment in the realization of her dreams. She is a survivor in the true sense of the word as she dares to face the hard realities of her life despite adverse circumstances and mounting odds with great courage, strength and determination. Each of Mukherjee's protagonists faces a different situation and has a different approach to life. These protagonists come to realize their problems and choose different means to solve them, but do not succeed to the same extent. They are not averse to confronting their problems and do not give in before them. In portraying their protagonists, the three novelists display contemporary feminine sensibility.

Since the publication of Desai's *Cry, The Peacock*, there has been a perceptible change in the aspirations of the Indian woman due to increasing influence of the West. Though the three novelists have disclaimed being feminists, the protagonists they portray are manifestations of a gradual change; these protagonists demonstrate the changing facets of Indian womanhood. Each faces a conflict between personal desires and societal expectations. Although they are not in a position to change the traditional male-oriented norms and codes, but they all at least dare to question them. Despite some differences, the three novelists agree on the need for self-determination for their protagonists. Their protagonists do get marginalized or perform their duties as per the whims and eccentricities of the male members in the family. They all seek their rightful place as human beings in society by refusing to be treated like doormat. They reject the socially defined role models for them. In spite of these similarities, the three novelists make their protagonists function differently. Anita Desai's protagonists seek a harmony that they cannot attain; Mukherjee's Jasmine alone is successful in creating her own harmony. But Shashi Deshpande's greatness lies in the fact that her protagonists seek and find harmony within the traditional social setup.

NOTES AND REFERENCES

1. Shashi Deshpande, "On the Writing of a Novel," *Indian Women Novelists*, Set I, Vol. 5, ed. R.K. Dhawan, New Delhi: Prestige Books, 1991, 34.

2. K. Meera Bai, "Feminism as an Extension of Existentialism: Women in Indian English Fiction," *The Commonwealth Review*, Vol. 6, No.1, 1994-95, 138.

3. K.R. Srinivas Iyengar, *Indian Writing in English*, New Delhi: Sterling, 1963, 464.

4. Veena Mathews, "Demythifying Womanhood," *The Times of India*, 25 September 1995, 138.

5. Anita Desai, Interviewed by Yashodhara Dalmia, *The Times of India*, 29 April 1979, 13.

6. ———, *Fire on the Mountain*, New Delhi: Allied, 1977, 3.

7. Shyam M. Asnani, "Desai's Theory and Practice of the Novel," *Perspective on Anita Desai*, edited by Ramesh K. Srivastava, Ghaziabad: Vimal, 1984, 5.

8. Anita Desai, *Cry, The Peacock*, New Delhi: Orient, 1980, 40.

9. *Ibid.*, 17.

10. *Ibid.*, 208.

11. *Ibid.*, 199.

12. *Ibid.*, 198.

13. *Ibid.*, 139.

14. Anita Desai, *Where Shall We Go This Summer?*, New Delhi: Orient, 1982, 99.

15. *Ibid.*, 139.

16. *Ibid.*, 144.

17. *Ibid.*, 145.

18. Anita Desai, *Fire on the Mountain*, 18.

19. ———, *Clear Light of Day*, London: Heinemann, 1980, 149.

20. *Ibid.*, 140.

21. Kamini Dinesh, "Fire on the Mountain: Negation of the Role Model," *Between Spaces of Silence*, edited by Kamini Dinesh, New Delhi: Sterling, 1994, 107.

22. Anita Desai, *Fire on the Mountain*, 17.

23. *Ibid.*, 30.

24. Anita Desai, *Where Shall We Go This Summer?*, 32.

25. *Ibid.*, 32.

26. *Ibid.*, 35.

27. *Ibid.*, 147.

28. Anita Desai, *Fire on the Mountain*, 133.

29. *Ibid.*, 143.

30. Anita Desai, *Clear Light of Day*, 140.
31. *Ibid.*, 156.
32. Anita Desai, *Fire on the Mountain*, 30.
33. ———, *Where Shall We Go This Summer?*, 32.
34. Bharati Mukherjee, *Jasmine*, India: Viking, 1990, 39.
35. *Ibid.*, 43.
36. *Ibid.*, 77.
37. *Loc. cit.*
38. *Ibid.*, 240.
39. Indira Nityanandam, *Three Great Indian Women Novelists*, New Delhi: Creative Books, 2000, 79.
40. Bharati Mukherjee, *Wife*, India: Penguin, 1990, 42.
41. Usha Bande, *The Novels of Anita Desai*, New Delhi: Prestige, 1988, 118-19.
42. Anita Desai, *Cry, The Peacock*, 208.
43. Bharati Mukherjee, *Wife*, 213.
44. Shashi Deshpande, *The Dark Holds No Terrors*, 62.
45. ———, "In Conversation: Sue Dickman with Indian Writers," *The Book Review*, Vol. XIX, No. 4., 1995, 33.

10
The Summing-up
————◆————

A close study of Shashi Deshpande's novels reveals her deep insight into the plight of Indian women, who feel smothered and fettered, in a tradition-bound, male-dominated society. She delineates her women characters in the light of their hopes, fears, aspirations and frustrations, who are aware of their strengths and limitations, but find themselves thwarted by the opposition and pressure from a society conditioned overwhelmingly by the patriarchal mind-set. She highlights their inferior position and the subsequent degradation in a male-dominated society.

Deshpande's women protagonists are victims of the prevalent gross gender discrimination, first as daughters and later as wives. They are conscious of the great social inequality and injustice towards them, and struggle against the oppressive and unequal nature of the social norms and rules that limit their capability and existence as a wife. Fettered to their roles in the family, they question the subordinate status ordained to them by society. Although she has a small volume of writing to her credit, her works have drawn great critical attention and acclaim for her sensitive and realistic representation of the Indian middle-class women. Her sincere concern for women and their oppressive lot is reflected strongly in all her novels.

In *Roots and Shadows*, Indu, the protagonist undergoes great mental trauma in her childhood and in marriage due to her husband Jayant's double standards. Ostensibly educated and liberal, he is intolerant about any deviation on her part from the traditional role of a wife. He is no different from the other less educated and conservative Indian men when it comes to playing the role of a husband. Besides, the miserable plight of Indu's *kaki*s and *atya*s is revealed to our gaze through Indu's eyes. The heart-rending account of *Akka*'s child marriage reveals the miserable condition Indian women of the older generation had to live in.

Shashi Deshpande has remarkably presented the inferior status of women by giving us an insight into the married lives of Indu's aunts and other relations. Although Indu is educated and has a liberal outlook, she realizes bitterly that her lot is no different from her numerous illiterate and village-bred aunts, and she too is a victim like them of the patriarchal social setup.

The Dark Holds No Terrors is a telling example of men who are intolerant about playing a second-fiddle role in marriage, and how their manhood gets hurt when their wives gain a superior status in society. Manu feels embarrassed and insecure with the rising status of his wife Saru and with it all the troubles start. But Deshpande has made society equally responsible for their deteriorating relations.

In *That Long Silence*, Jaya's troubles in marriage stem from her husband's intolerance towards any deviation from her role of a subservient wife. When threatened with charges of corruption, he expects her to go into hiding with him, which she refuses to comply with. He is greatly enraged and walks out of the house. Jaya is very confused and miserable as she had all along followed her Vanita *mami*'s advice that a husband is like a 'sheltering tree' which must be kept alive at any cost, for without it the family becomes unsheltered and vulnerable. She does so but finds herself and the children the more unsheltered and insecure.

In *The Binding Vine*, Shashi Deshpande raises the issue of hitherto untouched issue of marital rape. Women like Mira, Urmi's mother-in-law, have to bear the nightly sexual assault by their husbands silently. Other women like Shakutai, her sister Sulu, Kalpana and her sister have their own sorry tales. Shakutai's husband is a drunkard and a good-for-nothing fellow, who leaves his wife and children for another woman. Kalpana is brutally raped by Prabhakar, Sulu's husband. Urmi takes up cudgels on Kalpana's behalf and the culprit is caught.

On the other hand is Urmi. Her husband is in navy and during his long absence she craves for some physical gratification. Her friendship with Dr Bhaskar provides her ample opportunity, but she never oversteps the boundaries chalked out in marriage. But the painful aspect to this is that this virtue of hers will remain unacknowledged by her husband.

A Matter of Time is yet another novel wherein the husband walks out on his family comprising the wife and three daughters. Sumi, the protagonist, is so shocked that she lapses into complete silence but, apparently tries hard to keep things normal for her daughters. Her desertion is a cause for great humiliation and mental trauma for her as it's not only a matter of great shame and disgrace but a bitter realization of being unwanted. Words of sympathy from relations fail to console her. She is self-respecting and takes up a job for herself and her daughters. Though Gopal, her husband, returns but she is a new Sumi now. She has coped with the tragedy with remarkable stoicism.

In *Small Remedies*, Shashi Deshpande has narrated the tragic tale of Savitribai Indorekar, doyenne of the Gwalior Gharana. She leads the most unconventional of lives, but undergoes great mental trauma because of the double standards practised in society. Right from her childhood she had sensed the gross gender discrimination in the society that had one set of laws for men and another for women. Madhu, too, is a victim of the double standards of society. She gets totally estranged by her husband Som after she naively discloses to him about her single act of physical intercourse before marriage, though Som has himself had a full-fledged physical relation with another married woman before marriage.

Another aspect to Deshpande's novels is the lack of cordial relation between a mother and a daughter: In *Roots and Shadows*, Indu's mother dies in childbirth hence a delineation of the mother-daughter relationship is not there. In *The Dark Holds No Terrors*, the mother-daughter relationship occupies the centrestage. Saru's mother's cold and indifferent attitude towards her develops a sense of antagonism in Saru towards her mother. She develops aversion to all the traditional values represented by her mother. Saru's experiences in her crucial years of puberty make her hate womanhood itself. The entire novel revolves round Saru's uncordial relationship with her mother. It is to cause displeasure to her mother that she takes up medicine as a career and later marries a man from outside her caste.

In *That Long Silence*, Jaya also does not have any cordial relationship with her mother, and in turn her mother also does not have any strong maternal feelings towards her daughter. It is her mother's disapproval that makes her agree to marry Mohan. Jaya, in her turn, has great attachment to her son, but does not have equal warmth towards her daughter. She hates her mother for not living up to the ideal role of the perfect mother. Like Saru, she tries to be as dissimilar as possible, rejecting her as a role model.

In *The Binding Vine*, we find Urmi's relation with her mother as direct and frontal. Her hostility towards her mother is evident from her angry tone and language she uses when speaking with her or about her to others. She hates her for having sent her to Ranidurg as a child to be brought up by her grandparents. Shakutai also has a love-late relationship with her daughter, Kalpana.

In *Small Remedies*, we find that Savitribai Indorekar's relationship with her daughter Munni is not so warm. Munni feels unwanted, unloved and rejected by her mother and she develops a feeling of aversion towards her or her identity. Her mother dissociates herself from her daughter and in turn, she too dissociates herself from her mother. Munni even goes to the extent of taking a new name, "Shailaja Joshi." Thus, in Shashi Deshpande's novels, "There is no mother who could serve as a model for the daughter."[1]

Shashi Deshpande's protagonists' quest for identity gets largely accentuated due to their frustrating experiences born of the prohibitive nature of the Indian patriarchal society. In her novels, the host of male characters—husbands, lovers, fathers and other relations—display different aspects of patriarchy and oppression. While the majority of the husbands are patriarchal in their approach, the older men, particularly the fathers, are broad-minded. Surprisingly, the male friends are "feminist" in their approach and sympathise with the protagonists' lot. Deshpande's male characters only serve to enable the protagonists to define their identities more fully.

Shashi Deshpande states that she does not "believe in a simple opposition of bad bad men and good good women. I don't believe the world is like that at all."[2] Thus, she has constructed motifs of patriarchy and oppression by employing the method of negation and affirmation. Her protagonists are victims of the Indian patriarchy and after initial submission resist the oppressive situation, thereby reflecting the author's view that a woman must assert herself within marriage to preserve her individuality.

Shashi Deshpande's view on marriage is different from what most of the Western feminists like Simone de Beauvoir, Germaine Greer and Kate Millett hold. In *The Second Sex*, Simone de Beauvoir writes, "It has been said that marriage diminishes man, which is often true, but almost always it annihilates woman."[3] Germaine Greer even goes to the extent of saying that women should not marry. Kate Millett is of the opinion that marriage reduces the status of women to a mere object for decoration and a tool of man's sexual gratification. But Deshpande never subscribes to the views of any feminist. Her ideology may not be of the type radical feminists hold but she has her own brand of feminism which, as Jaidev says, "has to be authentic, rooted and context-bound."[4] And Deshpande is not against the institution of marriage, as her woman protagonists strive to make their marriages work in their endeavour to lead a meaningful existence.

Shashi Deshpande keeps her narratives female-centred and gives an intimate insight into the psyche of the middle-class Indian women who feel oppressed and hemmed in by their patriarchal socialization. She provides new ideals for a better man-woman relationship, thereby broadening the scope of woman's existence. She not only presents a feminist insight into patriarchal values, but also prescribes a balance between tradition and modernity as a working philosophy for the contemporary woman. To her, tradition are the values of harmony and coexistence that symbolize the Indian way of life, and modernity is the assertion of the independent, individual identity. After having passively played out their socially ordained roles, her protagonists move out of their cloistered selves to assert their individuality as human beings.

Deshpande feels that the woman must be true to her own self if she wants to realize herself. The straitjacketed role imposed on woman only bogs her down in mire of negation and suppression. She must venture out of the familial framework to give full expression to her individuality and identity.

Although she is not an avowed feminist, Shashi Deshpande occupies a place of pre-eminence among the contemporary woman novelists concerned with women's issues. Deshpande's creative talent and ideology have established her as a great feminist writer genuinely concerned with women's issues and anxieties. Her protagonists are modern, educated, middle-class women who, fettered to their stereotypical roles of a wife and mother, feel smothered and helpless in a tradition-bound male-dominated society.

Shashi Deshpande's novels are a realistic depiction of the anguish and conflict of the modern educated middle-class women. Caught between patriarchy and tradition on the one hand, and self-expression, individuality and independence on the other, her protagonists feel themselves lost and confused and explore ways to fulfil themselves as a human being. Deshpande's concern and sympathy are essentially for the woman. She has given an honest portrayal of her fears, sufferings, disappointments and frustrations. Besides revealing the woman's struggle to secure self-respect and self-identity, the author lays bare the multiple levels of oppression, including sexual oppression. Deshpande's primary concern for the woman makes her a feminist writer.

Undoubtedly Shashi Deshpande is a feminist writer but with a broad humanistic outlook. Her novels are essentially reflective of the unenviable situation of the beleaguered contemporary Indian women, which she has depicted with great artistic finesse and astounding originality. Her commendably realistic depiction of the contemporary Indian women's situation and the pragmatic solution she puts forward, accord her novels an imperishable importance for their affirmative eloquent message for women and the whole humanity as well.

NOTES AND REFERENCES

1. Adele King, "Shashi Deshpande: Portraits of an Indian Woman," *The New Indian Novel in English: A Study of the 1980s*, ed. Viney Kirpal, New Delhi: Allied, 1990, 164.

2. Shashi Deshpande, "Interview: Shashi Deshpande Talks to Lakshmi Holmstrom," *Wasafiri*, No. 17, Spring, 1993, 22.

3. Simone de Beauvoir, *The Second Sex*, translated and ed. H.M. Parshley, Harmondsworth: Penguin, 1983, 496.

4. Jaidev, "Problematising Feminism," *Feminism and Recent Fiction in English*, ed. Sushila Singh, New Delhi: Prestige Books, 1991, 57.

BIBLIOGRAPHY

Adhikari, Madhumalati, "The Female Protagonist's Journey from Periphery to Center: Shashi Deshpande's *The Intrusion and Other Stories,*" *Indian Women Novelists,* Set III, Vol. 4, edited by R.K. Dhawan, New Delhi: Prestige Books, 1995.

Ahuja, Suman, Rev. of *That Long Silence, Times of India,* 8 Oct. 1989.

Alphonso-Karkala, John B., *Indo-English Literature in the Nineteenth Century,* Mysore: University of Mysore, 1870.

Anandalakshmi, S., "The Female Child in a Family Setting," *The Indian Journal of Social Work,* Vol. LII, No. 1, January 1991.

Arora, Neena, *Nayantara Sahgal and Doris Lessing: A Feminist Study in Comparison,* New Delhi: Prestige Books, 1991.

Asnani, Shyam M., "Desai's Theory and practice of the Novel," *Perspective on Anita Desai,* edited by Ramesh K. Srivastava, Ghaziabad: Vimal, 1984.

Awasthi, A.K., "The Quest for Identity in The Novels of Shashi Deshpande," *Language Forum,* Vol. 18, No. 1, 1992.

Bai, K. Meera, "Feminism as an Extension of Existentialism: Women in Indian English Fiction," *The Commonwealth Review,* Vol. 6, No. 1, 1994-95.

Bande, Usha, "Tolerance or Female Altruism—A study of Shashi Deshpande's *A Matter of Time,*" *Language Forum,* Vol. 24, No. 1-2, 1998.

Bande, Usha, Rev. of *A Matter of Time, Indian Books Chronicle,* Mar.-Apr. 1997.

Bande, Usha, *The Novels of Anita Desai,* New Delhi: Prestige, 1988.

Barche, G.D., "Indu: Another Sisyphus in *Roots and Shadows,*" *Indian Women Novelists,* Set I, Vol. 5, edited by R.K. Dhawan, New Delhi: Prestige Books, 1991.

Beauvoir, Simone de, *The Second Sex*, translated and edited by H.M. Parshley, Harmondsworth: Penguin, 1983.

Bharvani, Shakuntala, "Some Recent Trends in Modern Indian Fiction: A Study of Deshpande's *That Long Silence*, Shashi Tharoor's *The Great Indian Novel* and Amitav Ghosh's *The Shadows Lines*," *Indian Women Novelists*, Set I, Vol. 1, edited by R.K. Dhawan, New Delhi: Prestige Books, 1991.

Bhatnagar, P., "*Indian Womanhood*: Fight for Freedom in *Roots and Shadows*," *Indian Women Novelists*, Set I, Vol. 5, edited by R.K. Dhawan, New Delhi: Prestige Books, 1991.

Bhatt, Indira, "That Long Silence: A Study," *Indian Women Novelists*, Set I, Vol. 5, edited by R.K. Dhawan, Delhi: Prestige Books, 1991.

——, "Shashi Deshpande's *The Dark Holds No Terrors*: A study in Guilt Consciousness," *Indian Women Novelists*, Set I, Vol. 4, edited by R.K. Dhawan, New Delhi: Prestige Books, 1991.

——, "*That Long Silence*: A Study," *Indian Women Novelists*, Set I, Vol. 5, edited by R.K. Dhawan, New Delhi: Prestige Books, 1991.

Bhavani, J., "*Nirdvandva*: Individuation and Integration as the Heroine's Quest in Shashi Deshpande's Fiction," *Indian Women Novelists*, Set III, Vol. 4, edited by R.K. Dhawan, New Delhi: Prestige Books, 1995.

Biswal, Aarti, "Sound of the Silenced: Shashi Deshpande's *That Long Silence*," *Revaluation*, Vol. 3, No. 1, 1997.

Chandra, Subhash, "City in the Novels of Kamala Markandaya, Anita Desai and Shashi Deshpande," *Indian Women Novelists*, Set I, Vol. 1, edited by R.K. Dhawan, New Delhi: Prestige Books, 1991.

——, "Silent No More: A Study of *That Long Silence*," *Indian Women Novelists*, Set I, Vol. 5, edited by R.K. Dhawan, New Delhi: Prestige Books, 1991.

Chandra, Suresh, "Feminist Aspects of Recent Fiction: Mahip Singh's *Who Walks With Me*, Kiran Nagarkar's *Seven Sixes are Forty Three* and Shashi Deshpande's *That Long Silence*," *Indian Women Novelists*, Set I, Vol. 1, edited by R.K. Dhawan, New Delhi: Prestige Books, 1991.

Chandra, Suresh, "Semiotics of Feministic Discourse in *That Long Silence*," *Critical Practice*, Vol. 3, No. 1, 1996.

———, "Woman's Liberation in the Fiction of Margaret Atwood and Shashi Deshpande," *Meerut Journal of Comparative Literature and Language*, Vol. 6, No. 2, 1993.

Chatterjee, Shoma A., "Shashi Deshpande: *Roots and Shadows*," *Amrit Bazar Patrika*, 2 Dec. 1984.

Choudhury, Romita, Interview with Shashi Deshpande. *World Literature Written in English*, Vol. 34, No. 2, 1995.

Daruwalla, Keki, "An Intense Book," Rev. of *That Long Silence. Indian Literature*, No. 146, Jan.-Feb. 1993.

Das, B.K., "Shashi Deshpande's *That Long Silence* and the Question of the Reader Response," *Indian Women Novelists*, Set III, Vol. 4, edited by R.K. Dhawan, New Delhi: Prestige Books, 1995.

David, Rubin, Rev. of *That Long Silence. Book Review*, May-June/July-Aug. 1989.

Desai, Anita, *Fire on the Mountain*, New Delhi: Allied, 1977.

———, Interviewed by Yashodhara Dalmia, *The Times of India*, 29 April 1979.

———, *Where Shall We Go This Summer?* New Delhi: Orient, 1982.

Deshpande, Shashi, "In Conversation: Sue Dickman with Indian Writers," *The Book Review*, Vol. XIX, No. 4, 1995.

———, "Interview: Shashi Deshpande Talks to Lakshmi Holmstrom," *Wasafiri*, No. 17, Spring 1993.

———, "On the Writing of a Novel," *Indian Women Novelists*, Set I, Vol. 5, edited by R.K. Dhawan, New Delhi: Prestige Books, 1991.

———, "An Archipelago," *Indian Review of Books*, Oct. 16-Nov. 15, 1993.

———, "Language No Bar," *Times of India*, 23 Apr. 1995, Ahmedabad.

———, "Literary Judgement," *Deccan Herald*, 4 Feb. 1995.

———, "Of Concerns, Of Anxieties," *Indian Literature*, Sep.-Oct. 1996.

Deshpande, Shashi, "The Dilemma of Women Writers," *Literary Criterion*, Vol. 20, No. 4, 1985.

——, "The Writing of a Novel," *Indian Women Novelists*, Set I, Vol. 5, edited by R.K. Dhawan, New Delhi: Prestige Books, 1991.

——, "Why I Write," *Kunapipi*, Vol. 16, No. 1, 1994.

——, Interviewed by Malini Nair, "The Message is Incidental," *Times of India*, No. 25, November 1989.

——, *It Was Dark*, Calcutta: Writers Workshop, 1986.

——, *It Was the Nightingale*, Calcutta: Writers Workshop, 1986.

——, *Roots and Shadows*, Madras: Sangam Books, 1983.

——, *Small Remedies*, New Delhi: Penguin, 2000.

——, *That Long Silence*, New Delhi: Penguin, 1989.

——, *The Hidden Treasure*, Bombay: Indian Book House, 1982.

——, *The Intrusion and Other Stories*, New Delhi: Penguin Books, 1993.

——, *The Legacy and Other Stories*, Calcutta: Writers Workshop, 1978.

——, *The Miracle and Other Stories*, Calcutta: Writers Workshop, 1986.

——, *The Narayanpur Incident*, Bombay: Indian Book House, 1982.

——, "The Dilemma of a Woman Writer," *The Literary Criterion*, Vol. 20, No. 4, 1985.

——, *The Binding Vine*, New Delhi: Penguin, 1992.

——, *The Dark Holds No Terrors*, New Delhi: Penguin, 1990.

Dhar, T.N., Rev. of *That Long Silence*, *Indian Book Chronicle*, Jan.-Feb. 1990.

Dinesh, Kamini, "Moving out of the Cloistered Self: Shashi Deshpande's Protagonists," *Margins of Erasure: Purdah in the Sub-continental Novel in English*, edited by Jasbir Jain and Amina Amin, New Delhi: Sterling, 1995.

Dwivedi, A.N., "The Hub of the Wheel: Some Recurrent Metaphors in Shashi Deshpande's Fiction," *Critical Practice*, Vol. 3, No. 1, 1996.

Fallis, L.S., Rev. of *The Dark Holds No Terrors, World Literature Today*, Vol. 55, No. 3, 1981.

Friedan, Betty, *The Feminine Mystique*, Harmondsworth: Penguin, 1971.

Futehally, Laeeq, Rev. of *The Binding Vine, Literature Criterion*, Vol. 28, No. 3, 1993.

Futehally, Shama, Rev. of *The Dark Holds No Terrors, New Quest*, 28 July-Aug. 1981.

Geeta, T.N., "The Story of Shashi Deshpande," *Indian Women Novelists*, Set. I, Vol. 5, edited by R.K. Dhawan, New Delhi: Prestige Books, 1991.

Geetha, T.N., Interview with Shashi Deshpande, *Indian Women Novelists*, Set III, Vol. 4, edited by R.K. Dhawan, New Delhi: Prestige Books, 1995.

Greer, Germaine, *The Female Eunuch*, St. Alabama: Paladin, 1976.

Guha, Ramchandra, "Not by Faith Alone," *The Sunday Express*, 1 October 1918.

Holmstrom, Lakshmi, "Of Love and Loss," Rev. *The Binding Vine, Indian Review of Books*, Oct. 16-Nov. 15, 1993.

Hunter College Women's Studies Collective: Women's Realities, Women's Choices: Introduction to Women's Studies, New Delhi: Oxford University Press, 1983.

Indira, S., "A Bond or Burden? A Study of Shashi Deshpande's *The Binding Vine*," *Indian Women Novelists*, Set III, Vol. 6, edited by R.K. Dhawan, New Delhi: Prestige Books, 1995.

Iyengar, K.R. Srinivas, *Indian Writing in English*, New Delhi: Sterling, 1963.

Jaidev, "Problematising Feminism," *Feminism and Recent Fiction in English*, edited by Sushila Singh, New Delhi: Prestige Books, 1991.

Jain, Jasbir (ed.), *Creative Theory: Writers on Writing*, Delhi: Pencraft International, 2000.

Jain, Madhu, "Sensitive Serving," Rev. of *That Long Silence, India Today*, 15 Sep. 1989.

Kerr, David, "History and the Possibilities of Choice: A Study of Anita Desai's *Baumgartner's Bombay*, Upamanyu

Chatterjee's *English, August* and Shashi Deshpande's *That Long Silence," Indian Women Novelists,* Set. 1, Vol. 1, edited by R.K. Dhawan, New Delhi: Prestige Books, 1991.

King, Adele, "Effective Portrait," *Debonair,* June 1988.

King Adele, "Shashi Deshpande: Portraits of an Indian Woman," *The New Indian Novel in English: A Study of the 1980s,* edited by Viney Kirpal, New Delhi: Allied, 1990.

King, Adele, Rev. of *The Binding Vine, World Literature Today,* Vol. 68, No. 2, 1994.

Lal, Malashri, "Good Luck to Entrepreneur," Rev. of *The Dark Holds No Terrors, Indian Book Chronicle,* 1 May 1981.

Mala R., "Sexual Predicament and Shashi Deshpande's Women," *Indian Women Novelists,* Set 1, Vol. 5, edited by R.K. Dhawan, New Delhi: Prestige Books, 1991.

Mathews, Veena, "Demythifying Womenhood," Novelist Shashi Deshpande talks to Veena Mathews, *Times of India,* 25 Sep. 1995, Ahmedabad.

Mathur, Malati, "Rebels in the Household," *India Today,* 3 April 2000.

Menon, K. Mahadevi, "The Crisis of Feminine: Shashi Deshpande's *That Long Silence," Commonwealth Quarterly,* Vol. 18, No. 46, 1993.

Millett, Kate, *Sexual Politics,* London: Rupert Hart Davis, 1971.

Moi, Toril, *Sexual/Textual Politics: Feminist Literary Theory,* London: Methuen, 1985.

Mukherjee, Bharati, *Jasmine,* India: Viking, 1990.

Mukherjee, Bharati, *The Tiger's Daughter,* London: Chatto and Windus, 1973.

Mukherjee, Bharati, *Wife,* India: Penguin, 1990.

Mukherjee, Meenakshi, "Ghosts from the Past," Rev. of *The Dark Holds No Terrors, Book Review,* Mar.-Apr. 1981.

Mukherjee, Meenakshi, "Sound of Silence," Rev. of *A Matter of Time, Indian Review Books,* 16 Mar.-15 Apr. 1997.

Mutalik-Desai, A.A., "Glint and Sparkle, Love and Death: Reflections on *Come Up and Be Dead," Indian Women Novelists,* Set. 1, Vol. 5, edited by R.K. Dhawan, New Delhi: Prestige Books, 1991.

Naikar, Basavaraj, "Joys and Sorrows of Womanhood in *The Binding Vine*," *Women in the Novels of Shashi Deshpande*, edited by Suman Bala, New Delhi: Khosla Publishing House, 2001.

Narayan, Shymala A., "Shashi Deshpande," *Contemporary Novelists* 5th ed., 1991.

Nityanandam, Indira, "Shashi Deshpande's *The Binding Vine*: Silent No More," *Indian Women Novelists*, Set I, Vol. 4, edited by R.K. Dhawan, New Delhi: Prestige Books, 1991.

——, *Three Greet Indian Women Novelists*, New Delhi: Creative Books, 2000.

Pal, Adesh, "*That Long Silence*: A Study of 'Displaced Anger,'" *Language Forum*, Vol. 21, No. 1-2, 1995.

Palkar, Sarla, "Breaking the Silence: *That Long Silence*," *Indian Women Novelists*, Set I, Vol. 5, edited by R.K. Dhawan, New Delhi: Prestige Books, 1991.

Pathak, R.S. (ed.), *The Fiction of Shashi Deshpande*, New Delhi: Creative Books, 1997.

Patil, Ujwala, "The Theme of Marriage and Self-hood in *Roots and Shadows*," *Indian Women Novelists*, Set I, Vol. 5, edited by R.K. Dhawan, New Delhi: Prestige Books, 1991.

Paul, Premila, "*The Dark Holds No Terrors*: A Woman's Search for Refuge," *Indian Women Novelists*, Set I, Vol. 5, edited by R.K. Dhawan, New Delhi: Prestige Books, 1991.

Plath, Sylvia, *The Bell Jar*, London: Faber & Faber, 1982.

Rajeshwar, M., "Trauma of a House-wife: A Psychological Study of Shashi Deshpande's *That Long Silence*," *Commonwealth Quarterly*, Vol. 17, No. 43, 1991.

Rama Rao, Vimla, Rev. of *That Long Silence Journal of Indian Writing in English*, Vol. 21, No. 1, 1993.

——, "A Well Articulated Silence," Rev. of *That Long Silence*, *Literary Criterion*, Vol. 27, No. 4, 1992.

——, "In Conversation with Shashi Deshpande," *Journal of Indian Writing in English*, Vol. 25, No. 1-2, 1997.

——, of *That Long Silence*, *Hindustan Times*, 6 May 1990.

——, Rev. of *That Long Silence*, *Tribune* (Sunday), 2 July 1989.

Ramamoorthi, P., "My Life is My Own: A Study of Shashi Deshpande's Women," *Indian Women Novelists,* Set I, Vol. 5, edited by R.K. Dhawan, New Delhi: Prestige Books, 1991.

——, "My Life is My Own: A Study of Shashi Deshpande's Women," *Feminism and Recent Fiction in English,* edited by Sushila Singh, New Delhi: Prestige Books, 1991.

Ramamurti, K.S., *Rise of the Indian Novel in English,* New Delhi: Sterling, 1987.

Rani, T. Asoka, "Feminism *vis-a-vis* Woman's Dignity: A Study of Shashi Deshpande's *That Long Silence," Journal of Indian Writing in English,* Vol. 24, No. 1, 1996.

Raveendran, P.P., "Beyond the Sheltering Tree: The Politics of Silence/Gaze in Shashi Deshpande's *That Long Silence," Critical Practice,* Vol. 4, No. 1, 1997.

Ravindra Prakash, "Becoming a Whole: A Reading of Shashi Deshpande's *The Dark Holds No Terror," Language Forum,* Vol. 18, No. 1, 1992.

Reddy, Y.S. Sunita, *A Feminist Perspective on the Novels of Shashi Deshpande,* New Delhi: Prestige Books, 2001.

Riti, M.D., "There's No Looking Back for Shashi Deshpande," An Interview, *Eve's Weekly,* June 16-29, 1988.

Sandhu, Sarbjit K., "The Image of woman in *Roots and Shadows," Indian Women Novelists,* Set I, Vol. 5, edited by R.K. Dhawan, New Delhi: Prestige Books, 1991.

——, "The Image of Woman in *That Long Silence," Indian Women Novelists,* Set I, Vol. 5, edited by R.K. Dhawan, New Delhi: Prestige Books, 1991.

——, "The Image of Woman in *The Dark Holds No Terrors," Indian Women Novelists,* Set I, Vol. 5, edited by R.K. Dhawan, New Delhi: Prestige Books, 1991.

——, *The Image of Woman in the Novels of Shashi Deshpande,* New Delhi: Prestige Books, 1991.

Sathupati, Prasannasree, "Conflict and Identity in Shashi Deshpande's Novels," *Indian Women Novelists,* Set III, Vol. 4, edited by R.K. Dhawan, New Delhi: Prestige Books, 1995.

Savio, G. Dominic, "A Woman's Heritage of the Commonwealth: A Study of *The Dark Holds No Terrors*," *Women in the Novels of Shashi Deshpande*, edited by Suman Bala, New Delhi: Khosla Publishing House, 2001.

Seshadri, Veena, Rev. *of That Long Silence, Literature Alive*, Vol. 1, No. 4, 1988.

Shirwadkar, Meera, *Image of Woman in the Indo-Anglian Novel*, New Delhi: Sterling, 1979.

Singh, Sushila, "Preface," *Feminism and Recent Fiction in English*, New Delhi: Prestige Books, 1991.

Stanley, Carvalho, "I'm Concerned with People," Interview with Shashi Deshpande, *Deccan Herald*, 27 Sep. 1989.

Sunder Rajan, Rajeshwari, "The Feminist Plot and The Nationalist Allegory: Home and World in Two Indian Women Novels in English," *Modern Fiction Studies*, Vol. 39, No. 1-2, 1993.

Suneel, Seema, *Man-Women Relationship in Indian Fiction* (With Focus on Shashi Deshpande, Rajendra Awasthi and Syed Abdul Malik), New Delhi: Prestige Books, 1995.

Swain, S.P., "Shashi Deshpande's *The Dark Holds No Terrors*: Saru's Feminine Sensibility," *Indian Women Novelists*, Set I, Vol. 4, edited by R.K. Dhawan, Delhi: Prestige Books, 1991.

——, "The Incarcerated Self and Derelict House," *Indian Literature*, Sep.-Oct. 1996.

Uma, Alladi, "Introduction: A Historical Background," *Woman and her Family, Indian and Afro-American: A Literary Perspective*, New Delhi: Sterling, 1989.

Venugopal, C.V. and M.G. Hegde, "Indian Women Short Story Writers in English: A Critical Study," *Indian Women Novelists*, Set I, Vol. 1, edited by R.K. Dhawan, New Delhi: Prestige Books, 1991.

Vishwanath, Vanamala, Interview with Shashi Deshpande, *Literature Alive*, Vol. I, No. 3, 1987.

Zutshi, Urmila, Rev. of *The Dark Holds No Terrors*, *Hindustan Times*, 14 Dec. 1980.

INDEX